Unafraid
Unashamed
In an Increasingly
Unfriendly World

Unafraid
Unashamed
In an Increasingly
Unfriendly World

Stanton G. Winder, Jr.
and
Kimberly Allston

Xulon Press

Xulon Press
2301 Lucien Way #415
Maitland, FL 32751
407.339.4217
www.xulonpress.com

Unless otherwise indicated, Scripture quotations taken from the English Standard Version (ESV). Copyright © 2001 by Crossway, a publishing ministry of Good News Publishers. Used by permission. All rights reserved.

Scripture quotations taken from the Holy Bible, New International Version (NIV). Copyright © 1973, 1978, 1984, 2011 by Biblica, Inc.™. Used by permission. All rights reserved.

Printed in the United States of America.

ISBN-13: 978-1-6628-1106-7

Dedication

"To my wife, Sue, who has been a faithful, loving partner, constant supporter, and ever a lover of the gospel"

Stanton G. Winder

"To Leah Sharibu, who is a living example of loving Christ over comfort."

Kimberly Allston

Foreword

Difficult days, division, polarization, malicious gossip, brutality of all stripes, gross selfishness, rampant greed. Sound familiar? It should. That is the cultural climate seeking to overwhelm a young Christian pastor... in the first century. What Timothy needed, and what God sent him, was the faith, patience, love, and perseverance of the gospel unpacked in a letter from the Apostle Paul. The church of Jesus Christ, in our cultural moment, needs to hear it all again.

Stanton Winder is a gift to the church as he leads us back into Paul's second letter to Timothy as a trusted and reliable guide. Stan is trusted, because for forty years of pastoral and educational ministry, Stan has been a faithful steward of this gospel of Jesus. His capacious appetite and keen mind for Scripture and history have always been in the service of ordinary Christians facing difficult days that 'proceed from bad to worse' (2 Tim 3:13). Stan is reliable, because in his own ministry and even in his own body, Stan is deeply and intimately acquainted with suffering. If the church in our day will live out our hope in the gospel and press this hope to our weary and suffering and broken neighbors, we need encouragement from a voice that knows the gospel deeply and knows how to suffer faithfully. Stan Winder is just such a voice. May the church be emboldened to compassion and courage and endurance as she hears him.

It's one thing to be led through the text to understand it. It's another thing to be led in applying that text in the context of our relationships — first in the Church, and then in the world. If the church is meant to be an outpost of the Kingdom of God in our world, we must be pressing together towards the fulness of that Kingdom in our relationships even now. And that means that we must refuse to rest content with what we know as all too common in our lives and our churches: surface relationships, divisive relationships, and casual acquaintances.

Kimberly Allston creates effective, comprehensive, gospel-centered devotionals, asking challenging, helpful questions that press readers towards each other in the body of Christ to concentrate on cultivating deep, authentic connections with Jesus, others, and themselves. Kimberly further bridges the gap between talk and walk by challenging, inspiring, and providing tools for believers to put the Gospel on display with their words and actions in all their relationships, both inside and outside the Church.

Luke Le Duc, Senior Pastor
Wheatland Presbyterian Church, Lancaster, Pa.

Introduction
"Shame Bombs"

How do Christians survive, much less thrive, amidst the endless lobbing of "shame bombs"? It seems that everywhere we Christians turn our values are being demeaned, marginalized, and delegitimized by social and broadcast media. Twitter takedowns and online bullying abound as angry taunts label us homophobic, sexist, and racist. We are the intolerant leftovers from the dark ages of the past. Do we not know that a new enlightenment has come, dispelling and overturning our antiquated, oppressive definitions of gender, marriage, moral absolutes, and societal norms? There is history to rewrite, a constitution to be "trashed," and a church to be silenced. There are death threats to be made, Twitter and Facebook posts to be taken down, and "hate-videos" to be crafted. The campaign to remake America has fired its opening salvo, and its verbal cannons have us squarely in their sights. *How then can we stand tall, unafraid, and unashamed in an increasingly unfriendly world?*

We can! Paul, the Apostle shows us the way as he delivers his swan song, his final letter, to his son in the faith, Timothy. As he writes, he knows what it means to be buried in an avalanche of shame and imminent cause for fear. For one, he, the "Founding Theologian" of the Church is *incarcerated*. Ever since Nero burned Rome and blamed the Christians for it in 64 A.D., it was not only demeaning, but it was also downright dangerous to be a Christian. Three years later, the aged apostle Paul was languishing in a dark, damp dungeon with only a hole in the ceiling for light and air.[1] The preliminary hearing of his case before the Roman Emperor Nero has already taken place. And apparently, no one stood as a witness for him. Now he is awaiting the full trial with *death looming* on the horizon. Suffering acutely from loneliness, hunger, the cold of prison life, tears come to his eyes. He is feeling the *abandonment* of a-number-of key people who have helped him in the past (1:15). How could they? Did he not give them two and a half years of his life! What is worse, some have even *turned away* from the gospel message. Others have *questioned* his authority as an apostle and still others have chosen to minister "below the radar."[2] Even his "son in the faith" — even Timothy — now faces the temptation to buckle under, to desert him, to walk away.

Surely his heart must cry out, "Stop Timothy! You can't do this Timothy! For Paul, time is running short. Who then will pass the faith along? What will happen to the churches he has established after he is gone? Already there is big trouble in the church of Ephesus in Asia (1:15). The most casual of observers can see the forces against the gospel closing in, persecution from without and heretics from within. Indeed, it may be that the young Christian church is teetering on the verge of extinction.[3] Will all his work go up in flames? Paul has every reason to be ashamed, to be afraid. But as you will see, he is not!

Why such boldness? The compelling reason for Paul's courage, amidst the most daunting of circumstances, is his obsession for preserving and handing down the life-giving Good News, this unfathomable treasure, to the ensuing generations. Indeed, that is his express purpose for writing. He is challenging and helping to create the same mindset in Timothy who would then create it in others. I can hear his

---

[1] Hendrickson, William, *New Testament Commentary: Exposition of the Pastoral Epistles*, (Grand Rapids: Baker Book House, 1968) p. 234.

[2] Constable, *Notes on Second Timothy*, p. 1.

[3] J.R. Stott, "The Message of Second Timothy," *The Bible Speaks Today*, (Leicester, England: Inter-Varsity Press, 1973) p. 21.

passionate pleadings, "O Timothy, guard it (1:14), suffer for it (2:3), remain faithful to it (3:14), proclaim it (4:2)! Give your life to getting "the Message" out!

Paul's fearlessness evokes the still vivid memory of my dad's bravery in a life-threatening situation. I can hear him yelling, "Stand still, don't move!" I had unknowingly walked into a "nest" of copperheads. As I stood paralyzed with fear, dad wielded his shovel, eliminating the threat.

That same intensity, that daring passion, that singularity of purpose is what fuels Paul as he proclaims, "I am not ashamed of the gospel!"

In a world where it is often a badge of honor to be ashamed of most everything Christian, Paul calls us to a higher commitment, to a dogged determination to live out and stand true to the gospel. And as he does, he will tell us why and he will show us how. We can be unashamed and unafraid in an increasingly unfriendly hostile world. So, let the journey begin!

As we begin our journey, we have divided the book into two parts to make this a fruitful endeavor.

Stanton Winder, in the chapters of *Part One* introduces, explains, and instructs in a concise way concerning the virtues and character of a shame-free life, as described in Second Timothy. With a strong voice, yet irenic spirit, he boldly, with grace and compassion, seeks to bring understanding and hope that will allow the reader to join Paul in proclaiming, "I am not ashamed!" Why? How?

In the face of fierce opposition, evangelical Christians have no reason to be ashamed, for: 1) The gospel is saturated with good news as God has directed and is guiding all of history toward a glorious triumphant end, free from every negative disastrous effect of sin, in a new heaven and new earth; 2) We have been given the best of life, best of family, highest of callings, the richest diversity, the greatest of gifts, and unlimited power to live a virtuous life; 3) Ours are the tools that cause us to rise above, rejoice in, and even see, the grand purpose in suffering and persecution; 4) We proudly embrace the new identity that is ours in

Christ; 5) We shudder at the shameful acts of shameful people, do battle with the enemy with the absolute assurance that the victory is ours, and yet are enabled and admonished to do it with a winsome, humble spirit; 6) We fear not for we are Spirit-enabled and Spirit-equipped to fulfill our marching orders; and 7) all along the journey, we get by with a little help and much more by our friends.

Kimberly Allston, in the devotionals of *Part Two*, helps you to take what you learn and have it become a source of inspiration, reflection, and day to day practice of this extraordinary "unashamed" life. She begins with a background summary of Paul's life that helps the reader understand his history and how Jesus influenced him to become, perhaps, the most noteworthy disciple to ever live.

After the background section, the devotions follow a pattern of sections to help the reader clearly understand the message of the chapters. The sections are *Verse(s), Challenge, Inspiration, God's Truth, Your Truth, and Action Plan*. With each verse highlighted, the reader is given a challenge to overcome. He or she is enabled to learn and grow from the understanding that we experience some of the very same challenges that Paul and Timothy had to overcome.

The inspiration section gives the reader an uplifting view of circumstances and obstacles that can strengthen us as followers of Christ. *God's Truth and Your Truth* helps the reader to understand the differences between his/her perspective and God's perspective. We are reminded that it is imperative that we compare His truth to our perceived truth. Finally, the *Action Plan* section gives the reader practical suggestions to help live out the scriptures and become more prepared as a discile in God's kingdom.

Will you come learn with us, grow with us, and walk with us on our journey?

Part One

■ ■ ■

Portrait of the Unashamed

Stanton G. Winder Jr.

Table of Contents

Chapter One
Ashamed of what?
2 Timothy 1:8

All of us have vivid memories associated with shame and shaming. Some shame is trivial and nonconsequential like a somewhat humorous moment in my childhood. There I was ready to run off to school except for one thing. I could not find my hat. I had looked everywhere. The bus was coming! I begged my mom to help me. But she just laughed. And the more I pleaded, her laugh became a "howl." You see, my hat was comfortably resting atop my head. Boy was I embarrassed!

Our humiliation can also be a self-affliction of quite serious circumstance. We are haunted by the shame and guilt of unkept promises, enslaving habits and unwise life-changing or even life-threatening decisions. Which reminds me. During my early years, I was immersed in a "gun-toting hunting culture." So, as I carried home my recently borrowed, unloaded, broken open shotgun. There was no cause for alarm until... I remembered I had to stop somewhere on the way home. As I opened the door, I stopped dead in my tracks. You see, I had entered my bank to cash a check. Thankfully, they knew me!

The shame Paul and Timothy faced was public disgrace on a much higher level. As his world saw it, Timothy had every reason to be ashamed. For one, his spiritual mentor was a prisoner "rotting away" in a dungeon (1:8,16). For another, Paul was incarcerated because of his obsession to proclaim worldwide the testimony concerning King Jesus. His world thought it to be a "message of a failed prophet, rejected by his people, executed by the world's power, and preached by a collection of fisherman and other undesirables."[4] Give your life to the propagation of this nonsense, risk your neck for this? What foolishness!

What they did not, and most today do not know, is the depth, breath, and beauty of this "testimony concerning our Lord." We call it the gospel, the good news. Majestic news which spans all of time and history and beyond! Our gospel message is so much more than Jesus being born in a manger and dying on the cross. Consider this:

1. Before God formed the galaxies or fashioned one planet, before He spoke creation into being, God was thinking of you. God chose to reach out to you! Yes, He knew we would engage in wrongdoing and fall prey to every imaginable form of destructive thinking, destructive habits, and destructive relationships. But right then, God the Father, Son and Holy Spirit designed a master plan to save and deliver the whole of creation from the coming devastation of sin.

2. Part of this plan was to choose the nation, Israel, from which would come the Messiah, the God-man Jesus, the Savior/Deliverer of the world. Imagine what wisdom, raw power and sovereign control was necessary to preserve that nation Israel through captivity and the oppression of the Babylonian, Persian, Greek, and Roman empires until Messiah Jesus was born.

3. Then God entered history in flesh and blood and lived among us. Your salvation demanded that someone live a perfect life in your place and take the fury of God's punishment for your every sin. Jesus did that! Proof positive that his work was satisfactory was God raising Him from the dead.

4. But the "good news" is even more than that! God has directed history and indeed your history, so that his saving message would be preserved (through the Scriptures) and one day be delivered by

---

[4] Mounce, William D. "Second Timothy," *Word Biblical Commentary: Pastoral Epistles*, Vol. 46, (Grand Rapids, Michigan: Zondervan, 2006) p. 1002 Adobe Digital Editions

someone directly to you. The one that chose you gave you the choice to choose him.

5. Daily, the ascended Jesus intercedes directly to God on your behalf and is designing and building you a future home. He has even sent God the Holy Spirit to live in you — guiding, empowering, transforming, comforting, strengthening, and walking you through the worst and best of life. You are becoming a new creation.

6. But best of all, some day He is coming back to bring heaven to earth. You who have trusted in Christ alone to save you — and have surrendered to him as your new boss — will forever enjoy a brand-new heaven and earth. Imagine a perfect world free from all pollution and disease of any kind. Imagine a body with no imperfections. Imagine lasting, unbreakable relationships. Imagine walking and talking face-to-face with God.

All this is the good news!!! Indeed, it is this indescribably amazing creation, and re- creation story that prompted Paul to loudly proclaim, **"I am not ashamed!"**

In the fall of 1959, I was seven, attending public school in one of the top school districts in the state of Pennsylvania. I loved school, especially history and science and, above all, my teacher, Mrs. Lehman. It was a great year, but one day sticks out above all others. We were studying Darwinian evolution. My teacher began to tell us that our ancestors were apes, that humans came from a long line of monkeys. "Was she kidding, I thought?" Immediately, I stood up and firmly said, "The Bible doesn't say that." The whole class froze. This was certainly a change to the regular classroom demeanor. She kindly asked me to sit down. But I just stood there and repeated, "The Bible doesn't say that." Understandably, I was again told that I must sit down immediately. I did. I had just experienced my first, "I am not ashamed" moment.

Chapter Two
Why No Shame?
2 Timothy 1:1-7

His face was downcast, and his voice quivered as he recalled the first day of philosophy class in a leading university. Bob's initial excitement had been abruptly terminated within the first few minutes of class. The professor, no sooner than having announced the title of the course, lifted high a Bible and exclaimed, "See this. This is a Bible." As the words left his mouth, he tossed the Scriptures halfway across the room. Then a dramatic pause. And now the chilling warning: "That is the last I want to hear of it in this class!" What am I to do, Bob asked me?

Over thirty years have passed since the incident, and what was then an anomaly is slowly becoming a societal norm. Noted contributor to the New York Times and Wallstreet Journal, Mary Eberstadt, documents this societal revolution.[5] Eberstadt chronicles the "new intolerance" of the "antichristian antagonists" in their frenzied, even crazed pursuit of what they denounce as "ideological Christian dissidents."[6] She decries their 'stalking and threatening of Christian pastors for being Christian pastors, the denigrating of social science that doesn't fit their ideology of what is a family, the telling a flight attendant she can't wear a crucifix... and their slandering and labeling millions by saying that people of religious faith hate certain people when they do not or are "phobes" of one stripe or another when they are not.'[7]

---

[5] Eberstadt, Mary, It's Dangerous to Believe: Religious Freedom and Its Enemies, (New York:Harper Collins,2016) Kindle.

[6] Ibid, 12-13.

[7] Ibid, 14.

Indeed, many of us took notice when a teacher lost her job for posting her beliefs against same sex marriage on Facebook, when a visitor to the National Gallery of Art was ordered to remove her pro-life pin because it was a religious symbol, when a U.S. Marine was court-martialed and denied benefits for posting Isaiah 54:17 near her office computer ("No weapons formed against me shall prosper.").[8] Recently we have found progressives labeling Christians as Nazis, Fascists, mentally ill and dangerous. Ironically, this almost daily shaming and blaming of Christians bears an eerie resemblance to the actual Nazi tactics used against Jews a generation ago.

So, what then do we do? *I suggest we start by refusing to be shamed.* We have every reason to be proud of the Gospel and nothing of which to be ashamed. Why no shame, you ask? First, we have the *promise of life that is in Christ Jesus.* (2 Tim 1:1 ESV). Ours is extraordinarily good news! "You can, you will, experience life at its best, beginning now and reaching its full richness and beauty in the world to come. As a fully devoted follower of Christ, Jesus is the very "habitat of eternal life."[9] We are forever united to him. We have been placed into his family, a most noble distinction. For we will one day reign as co-regents with him over the earth (2:12). By living in union with Christ, we know what it means to have life and to live that life to the "extreme." No cause for shame here!

Second, we have a *forever* family in the "body" of Christ. In a culture plagued by dysfunctional and fractured families, ours will endure throughout the ages. This is no ordinary family, but brothers and sisters, the epitome of diversity, from every race, every language and every nation bonded in a unified whole. And what does life in this prestigious family look like?

---

[8] Ibid, 78ff.

[9] Gundry, Robert H., Commentary on First and Second Timothy, Titus (Baker Academics: Grand Rapids, Michigan, 2010) p. 48, Adobe Digital Editions

In our good days, and not so good days, our Christian family prays for us and goes to bat for us. Paul says to his spiritual son Timothy, *I remember you constantly in my prayers, night and day* (1:3 ESV). We can only imagine what darkness brought to that filthy pit in which Paul spent his nights. But instead of immersing himself in self-pity, he immersed himself in prayer. If he could not be with his "son" Timothy in person, he could be with him in heart. Every one of us knows someone in "the family" that never stops banging on the door of heaven for us. For over fifty years, every day throughout the day, my mom did that.

Paul continues. *As I remember your tears, I long to see you* (1:4a ESV). He daily felt the pain of their parting. Our Christian family shares our tears with us — tears of parting, tears for losses, tears of sharing our joys, and tears flowing over our failures. We are never alone in our humiliation and we are never alone in our jubilation. We have the family!

Most importantly, it is this family that passes down the faith to us. By family I mean not only biological descendants, but the larger family of sincere, life-breathing, life-giving believers since the origin of time. They are our spiritual heritage. Have we not great roots!

Timothy was blessed to be a third generation Christian. *I am reminded,* says Paul, *of your sincere faith, a faith that dwelt first in your grandmother Lois and your mother Eunice and now, I am sure, dwells in you as well* (1:5 ESV). Mom and Grandma had been Jewish converts who faithfully studied the Old Testament Scriptures and saw Christ as the Messiah for whom they and their ancestors had prayed and longed for. As a result, Timothy, from his infancy, was immersed in the teachings and life application of the OT Scriptures. He had mastered the Torah. The stories of Noah, Moses, Rebekah, Samson, David, Solomon, Ruth, Isaiah, Jonah, Daniel, and Esther ever lived in his heart and mind, ever influencing his life goals and actions. Third, we have God-given gifts and a God-directed calling. No reason for embarrassment here! Whatever the profession or vocation you are engaged in (homemaker, farmer, doctor, mechanic, pastor, educator, business leader, etc.) you are in Christian work, an emissary sent and equipped (gifted) for that mission by the King of Kings. Through the most menial and the most monumental of tasks you are God's workmen and workwomen living "The Message" by word and by deed.

Paul encourages Timothy *to fan into flame the gift of God which is in you through the laying on of my hands, for God gave us a spirit not of fear but of power and love and self- control.* (1:6-7 ESV). And so, He encourages you:

1) Stoke the inner fire; set it ablaze.

2) Constantly be working at bringing the special gift(s) God has given you to their full potential.[10] Whether God has called and equipped you to serve others, teach others, or lead others, be exceptionally generous or merciful to others; stay at it. As Lea writes, "The command does not imply that Timothy had let his spiritual flame go out. It is an appeal for continual vigorous use of his spiritual gifts."[11] (For Timothy, there was a memorable time when these pastoral gifts had been recognized and confirmed through the process of ordination.)

3) Do not be a coward; do not flee the battle!

Paul reminds us that cowardice has no place in Christianity. For God's Spirit does not create in us a spirit of fear. God never gives a task to do without affording us everything necessary to do it. He gives boldness when we want to run and hide from our duties. He gives us power when the task is daunting or overwhelming, and its completion seemingly impossible. He gives us unconditional and extravagant love when people seem overly annoying or we are tempted to take credit and to

---

[10] Mounce, p. 995.

[11] Lea, Thomas, D, and Wayne P. Griffin Jr, "First and Second Timothy, Titus", *The New American Commentary* (Nashville, Tennessee: B&R Publishing Co., 1992) p. 195, Adobe Digital Editions

be self-serving. He gives us self-control when we are prone to be harsh, impulsive, and lack wise judgment. Just ask!

Indeed, it would be foolish — for those who have the best of life, the best of family, the highest of callings, and the greatest of gifts — to cower in shame. We were made for another world that will shine in its brilliance and display forever its purity when this decaying, dying world is gone and forgotten. Can you say with me, "I am not ashamed!"

Chapter Three
Suffering's No Shame!
2 Timothy 1:8-14

I remember well the shame, "the mark of disgrace," I felt the first time I had to use a wheelchair for long distances. I had joined the minority class labeled "disabled." Soon after followed the raised voices from those strangers who addressed me, speaking slowly to account for what they perceived to be my diminished capacity to hear or understand. Had I suddenly grown hard of hearing? Was I now suffering from cerebral dementia? Certainly not!

But was this wounding of my pride really a big deal? No! Indeed, the humiliation of the disease dimmed, even disappeared, when contrasted with the shame of another sort. And I gladly bear that disrespect as a badge of honor.

You see, I have been for years a member of another minority class labeled "evangelical Christian." There is and has been a stigma, an undeserved humiliation, even suffering, that falls upon those who are called by that name. Does that surprise us? Of course not! It is easily the summation of our founder's life on earth, climaxing in the unconscionable degradation of the cross. As John Piper writes, "Shame was stripping away every earthly support that Jesus had: his friends gave way in shaming abandonment; his reputation gave way in shaming mockery; his decency gave way in shaming nakedness; his comfort gave way in shaming torture; His glorious dignity gave way to the utterly undignified, degrading reflexes of grunting and groaning and screeching." [12]

You see, suffering loses its shame when we discover that we really begin to know Christ when we experience some of the same sorrows He tasted in life, and when we are willing to face death for Him as He faced death for us. As I have written elsewhere, "Suffering is God's tool to allow us the privilege of *sharing in the sufferings of Christ* with the promise of getting to know him even better (Philippians 3:10). We can never really know all that Christ went through, all that He suffered, when He laid aside the trappings of glory to travel the trail of tears for us. But when we are *misunderstood*, we are reminded that He was misunderstood. When we are *maligned*, when we are *misquoted*, when we are *marginalized*, when we are *ostracized*, and when we are *persecuted*, we begin to understand the depths to which He plunged to deliver us from sin, separation and Satan. And if we are called to *give our lives* for Him, we will be given an even better glimpse of the enormity of the task, the infinitude of a love that would stop at nothing less than the ultimate sacrifice to give us the ultimate best, an eternity with Him. Is it not worth all our pains and sorrows to share, however small it is, in His?"[13] To suffer for Him is to truly know Him.

Twice, Paul urges Timothy to not be ashamed, but instead to join with other Christians in suffering for the gospel (1:8, 2:3). As Hebrews 13:3 challenges us, we are to actively care and respond to those who are imprisoned, mistreated, and persecuted for the gospel's sake. How fitting this is when the last one hundred years has seen more martyrs than in all the centuries before it.

But how do we endure, how do we rise above the shame of suffering? First, there is no end to the power God can provide us! He can give

---

[12] https://www.desiringgod.org/articles/what-does-it-mean-for-jesus-to-despise-shame

[13] Winder Jr, Stanton G, and Kimberly Allston. *When Faith Is All There Is: Faith Is Enough*, (Amazon, 2017) p. 47.

us the **power** to endure any, and all suffering (1:8). Proof positive of God's omnipotence is the transformative power displayed in initiating and enabling Christians to live a holy life (1:9). Through Christ He has broken the stranglehold of sin on our life (Rom. 6:6-7, 14). Where once destructive enslaving habits reigned supreme, we have now been set free to follow a new calling, to fulfill a divine personal invitation to live a sanctified life. We find ourselves spreading the truth instead of spreading lies, building up instead of tearing down, and loving selflessly instead of loving selfishly. The God who saved us from the penalty of sin now delivers us from the power of sin.

Further, there is the stunning display of divine power in that Jesus has demolished death (1:10). Christ has rendered completely powerless the fear of the certainty of death. He defeated *physical* death by rising again with a new glorified body. So, we too will rise and live again. He removed the punishment of death *spiritually*, for in His death He paid in full the punishment our sin demanded. He ended the threat of *eternal* death, for we can never again be separated from God. Because He lives, we can face tomorrow. All fear is gone. All has been forgiven. So, when we shudder at the prospect of losing our life, having our character impugned, our family assaulted, or our faith denied, we are reminded that Christ conquered the greatest enemy of all. Christ conquered death. All other enemies pale into insignificance in comparison to this.

> Remember now — the one penning these words is at the very door of death. These are not trivial musings or philosophical babble. At any moment Paul's cell door could be opened, and he would be marched down the road to the place of his execution. Soon his head would be severed from his body. Yet, he stands defiant, for death was only a door that opened immediately into the very presence of his Lord. He is not ashamed to be counted a criminal for the cause of Christ

Indeed, so great is God's power that we can be fully convinced of the certainty of God's ability to preserve and guard both the truth of the Gospel and the soul and ministry of the one who proclaims it, until Christ comes back again (1:12, 14). One day the message you preach and the life you live will be proven to be right. You are the proud recipients of a priceless treasure which has been deposited for safekeeping with Christ's church. And not only is this a priceless treasure, a good deposit, but the words of the gospel are, "sound words or healthy words (trustworthy, healing words)."[14]

Timothy is to model the sound teaching he has heard from the apostle. Why? There are heretics bent on corrupting this gospel and robbing the church of this priceless gift. They want to refine, redefine, update, soften, harden, and add to the gospel. Sound familiar?

But you say, "Wait a minute! How am I supposed to do this?" Answer! Put your trust in Christ who will help you keep the deposit safe. He will do what I cannot do for me. I further put my trust in the indwelling, divine resident teacher, the Holy Spirit who both leads you to the gospel truth and forever preserves that truth. Bottom line, God is the guarantor of the gospel.

God will never allow the light of the gospel to be totally extinguished. We have the threefold enablement and guarantee of the Trinity. Yes, we must play our part in guarding and defending the truth, but God has not taken his hands off it. He is the final guardian, and he will preserve the truth which he has committed to the church.

Today Christians face many head-on who are strong opponents to the Gospel. We live in a postmodern world that entirely rejects absolute truth. "It may be true for you, but it is not true for me," they say. We confront atheism at every turn, which denies the existence of the supernatural; agnosticism, which isn't sure if there is a God; and a scientific world enslaved to various forms of evolutionary thought. We hear every

---

[14] See Stott, 43-44 and Mounce, 1016-17

day of those who would ban our religious expression from the marketplace and confine it to within the halls of the church or the walls of the home. But perhaps our greatest enemies are those who distort or reinvent the Gospel. Now what exactly does that look like? What do we need to guard against?

Here are a few examples of current false views:

Religious pluralism — There are many roads to God. Different religions are equally valid and acceptable ways to knowing God. We would agree that there are elements of truth in all religions, but only Christ provides the way of salvation — the ultimate solution to the human dilemma. There is only one true Gospel.

1. *Easy-believism* — This is the idea that people can simply pray the sinner's prayer and are forever saved, even if there is nothing in their lives afterwards that suggests true repentance or surrender to Christ as their new master and Lord. We agree that genuine believers are forever kept by the love and power of God (Rom. 8:31-39). But true authentic faith and repentance will result in bearing the fruit of the Spirit and conformity to the character of Christ. A flippant attitude about forsaking sin in one's life is a mark of one who professes but does not actually possess Christ.

2. *Un-biblical views of Christ's person* — Some deny that Christ was God or fully God and others that Christ was fully human. Others deny the unity of the divine and human natures in one person, or the distinction between the two natures. The Scriptures teach that Jesus was one person with both a divine and human nature. He was fully God and fully man.

3. *Political gospel* — Some practice, even though they would not necessarily believe, that a political solution is the primary need for our nation's problems. Some would even equate Christianity

with a political party. In the end, we cannot assume that a type of government or a certain party is the solution to our problems. Only Christ can, and will, bring in the perfect rule and government that the world desires (Isaiah 9:6).

4. *Prosperity gospel* — This is the idea that the gospel guarantees the power to be free from all diseases and poverty. We would agree that the healing work of God marvelously, even miraculously, reveals itself often — in both providing for needs and delivering us from our diseases. Certainly, we have been completely and fully delivered spiritually from the effects of sin, death, and the devil. But we are not guaranteed to be rich or to be healthy simply because we are a Christian.

5. *Feel Good gospel* — This is the idea that we do not want to make people feel bad about themselves by proclaiming the idea of an eternal hell. But we cannot pick and choose the parts of the Gospel message that make us feel good or that we like. Jesus mentions hell more than any other New Testament writer.

6. *Gospel of legalism* — J. I. Packer defines legalism as, "belief that one's labor earns God's favor, that good deeds are essentially ways to earn more of God's favor."[15] This graceless salvation enslaves a person to a fulfillment of a list of do's and don'ts, produces arrogance in those who feel they have mastered the list, and ends in love-less-ness as their "professed righteousness" squeezes humble kindness and creative compassion out of the heart.[16]

Second, God has a profound **grand purpose** in both the suffering of His Son and your suffering. Paul says that Jesus not only incapacitated

---

[15] Packer, J. I., *Concise Theology*, (Carol Stream, Illinois: Tyndale House Publishers, 1993) pp. 175-6.

[16] See *Counterfeit Gospels: Rediscovering the Good News in a World of False Hope* by Trevin Wax for a good discussion of the various false views in today's world.

death through the cross, but He illuminates — shows the way to life and immortality through both His resurrection and our sharing of the Good News (1:10). Where the certainty and nature of life after death was once shrouded in darkness, Christ's post-resurrection appearances proved the reality of a "forever life" beyond the grave.

Gladly we struggle, even endure persecution and suffering, to light up our world with the assured truth that where there is death, there is the promise of life to come; and where there is hopelessness, there is the hope of a grand new world where all will be right.

Paul closes the chapter (1:15-18) by giving examples of those who are unashamed and loyal to the gospel and those who are shamed and unfaithful to the gospel. It seems that the defections by "Christians" in Ephesus (and in the province of Asia where Ephesus stood) are so numerous and widespread that Paul could say all have turned from him (Paul names two of the ringleaders, Phygelus and Hermogenes.). This seems to be more than just deserting Paul but is also a disavowal of his apostolic authority, and with it the apostolic message.[17]

But there is one bright exception in the person of Onesiphorus. Paul remembered the precious and numerous times of being entertained in his home and refreshed by his company. He specifically notes that he had not been ashamed of Paul's chains, but had even travelled to Rome and searched diligently for Paul until he found him in his dungeon prison. That was risky business! Accordingly, Paul offers up a prayer of blessing for his household and hopes that he will find mercy from the Lord when he stands before Christ's Judgment Seat (2 Cor. 5:10).

Paul, it seems, envisions these believers standing before the Lord with God noting the failure and faithlessness of some, while Onesiphorus escapes such shame and instead receives mercy and a commendation. Paul is implying that Timothy would be wise to

---

[17] Fee, Gordon D., "1 and 2 Timothy, Titus," *New International Biblical Commentary* (Peabody, Massachusetts: Hendrickson Publishers, 1993) p. 236 and Stott, p. 45.

follow the example of Onesiphorus.[18] Sometimes we need a gentle prodding, a loving rebuke. Sometimes we need a reminder that suffering is a badge not a blemish, a privilege not a shame.

I had just heard the news, "You have a cancerous tumor in your throat…You will undergo 25 radiation treatments during the next month. Then we will re-evaluate."

It was scary, but soon a peace flooded my soul. I turned my eyes toward heaven and prayed, "Lord, certainly I want to be healed, but that will not be my first petition. What I ask is that you will so control me that *I will be a light,* a testimony to the world around me." I largely kept that request to myself. Only a couple of people knew.

The next weeks were tough. My mouth, throat and esophagus were filled with ulcers. I lost weight from my inability to eat any solids. If I did try to eat, searing pain would follow, and literally everything tasted like ink. Yet throughout, God put a smile on my face and praise regularly poured from my mouth; and I survived on five nutritional shakes a day.

During that month he graciously enabled me to speak five times over a forty-eight-hour-period at our SC Anglican Diocesan Youth Conference, EPIC. The words came out so powerfully, even though I was in such pain and could hardly function. Indeed, the first night I told my wife, Sue, that I did not know if I would be able to speak. Then God intervened. Over the next thirty minutes, the pain was lifted. It would return with a vengeance as soon as I was through. But God's abiding presence never left me. It was the most memorable conference of my life.

Then came the day when my treatments were over, and I would "ring the bell" indicating that I was cancer-free. As the technician walked with me down the hall, he stopped me and said, "Stan you have been a light to everyone around you here, the doctors, nurses, technicians and all the other staff." My eyes teared up; God had answered my prayer. God so often does His greatest work as we walk through the fires of affliction.

---

[18] Constable, *Notes on Second Timothy,* p. 13.

Chapter Four
Be Strong: Embrace your Identity!
2 Timothy 2:1-13

Our shame culture does not simply attack us for wrongful acts which we have done; it strikes at the core of who we are. It is more the beliefs that form our identity than our behaviors that are under assault. We are the "basket of deplorables" — "din-wits," whose gospel makes us gay-haters, female suppressors, and arrogant exclusivists claiming to have cornered the market on divine inspiration and truth. There is no way out, they tell us, no possibility of removing this garment of shame except to abandon our faith altogether. To be indicted is to stand convicted.

What then is the path to weather this storm? *To begin, embrace, do not try to erase, your identity.* Your strength is found in who you are. First, *you are a* **child of the King of Kings** who will one day demolish the kingdoms and destructive philosophies of this world (2:1). You will reign with Him! You are royalty. And He shall reign forever and ever (Rev. 11:15). The grace that broke the chains of darkness over you in the past is the same grace that each day empowers and enables you to not be ashamed of who you are. Your power source is the relationship you have with Jesus Christ and the Holy Spirit who indwells you.

Second, *you are an* **ambassador of the King**, *passing on the gospel news of your indomitable faith to others.* There is strength in numbers. Let them, too, embrace the unshakeable identity you have as a member of Christ's body — His community the church (2:2). Do not keep this news to yourself. This is not only a singular responsibility but a corporate responsibility. We all are to pass the faith along from one generation to another. (Here, Paul's focus is on Timothy choosing ministers (elders) who are trustworthy: 1) in both their godly, Christ-like character and 2) in their fidelity to the apostle's teaching and ability to also teach others.)

Third, *you are **good soldier**, empowered to endure and persistent to prevail in suffering* (2:3-4). The Christian has a wholehearted single-minded devotion to carrying out the orders of His commander, King Jesus. We are here to please the One in whose army we serve and pays our wages. We are committed to remaining free from any entanglement, any distraction, and to avoid taking any detour that would endanger a victory. This will undoubtably bring insults and defamation; and will enlist persecution by the enemies of Christ and His gospel. But the Christian soldier is steadied by the assurance of a future reward in heaven (Matt. 5:11,12) and ultimate victory at Christ's coming (2 Thess. 1:5-8). They are ever reminded that the way is narrow, through Jesus alone, and the journey hard that leads to eternal life. Yes, the path that the gospel deniers take may be easy and wide, accommodating the crowd with all its baggage, but the end of that road brings destruction and eternal separation from God (Mat. 7:13-14).

Fourth, *a fully devoted, follower of Christ is a **winning athlete** who will wear a crown at the end of life's race* (2:5). All the blood sweat and tears of both training and competition, and all the attention and self-discipline given to participating according to the rules will be worth its weight in gold someday. Our rules are the moral teachings of Christ and the Scriptures — the Great Commission and the Great Commandment (Matt. 18:19, 20; Matt. 22:37-40). We cannot accept the ones we like — the ones that are popular — and consequently reject the ones that bring on the seething hatred and contemptuous derision of the sadly misinformed — the misunderstanding, unbelieving crowd. We cannot look back; we will not let up until we cross the line.

Fifth, *our identity is found in our **solid work ethic***. We are like **hard-working farmers** who from sunset to sundown can be found planting the seed, cultivating, weeding, spraying and finally harvesting a crop

(2:6). All this is done facing the unknowns of losing that crop due to weather, disease and/or animals. But tenaciously we plod on knowing that the hard-working farmer receives the first share of the crops. The seeds we plant are the life-giving truths of Scripture that can rescue the fallen world from destructive habits, deceptive teachers, and damning judgement. The reward is to see people come to the faith and the amazing transformation of hope and character that follows.

Sixth, *our identity is found in that we are the **confident propagators** of a trustworthy message that cannot be silenced* (2:8-13). Even as Christian values and beliefs are being blocked on social media, we are reminded that ultimately our message must and will prevail. When we suffer, we do not suffer for nothing. *There are certain insurmountable, foundational, life-changing realities that frame and focus our Gospel message:*

1) *Jesus Christ as the very God has conquered death and the grave. Jesus as a perfect man is of the line of King David, the Messiah-King that was long promised.* His unstoppable power assures our own victory over death, and His regal blood the consummation and splendid glory of the eternal kingdom which was promised us (2:8).

2) *The messengers of the good news may be shackled and bound, but the message can never be bound.* In every age, the enemies of the cross have beaten, raped, plundered, and killed its soldiers, only to find the light of the gospel emerge burning more brightly than ever before. Indeed, it is because of intense sufferings by Paul that the salvation of many was accomplished (See II Cor. 11:16-33). It is through the stained-glass window of his misery that the glimpse of the coming glory shone through (2:9-10).

3) *We have died in Christ to our old way of life; we are empowered by Christ to live in newness of life.* In the mind of God, when Christ died on the cross, we, too, died with Him. And when He rose again, we, too, have risen in Him. Romans 6:1-14 explains what all this

means. Our "old self" — which was enslaved, dominated, ruled by the sinful nature inherited from Adam — has been set free from sin's tyranny and resultant death. By the power of the resurrection and the indwelling, sanctifying Holy Spirit, we are free — free at last. Not only is there a compunction toward the failed practices of the past, but there is a God-implanted (Spirit-propelled) desire to increasingly adopt the moral profile, passions, and purposes of Jesus Christ.[19] (2:11) Yes it is true that Christians fall, fail, and even, for a moment, forsake living a holy life. But "we will continue to repent, never acquiescing, never making excuses, never surrendering, but ever desiring to be further changed into Christ's image."[20]

4) *As we endure suffering and temptation now, we are reminded that we will one day be rewarded by reigning with Christ throughout all eternity.* We live in the now with a purpose and irresistible pull toward the future, and what a future it is! This truth that "we are kings and queens in Christ", that we will one day judge angels (1 Cor. 6:3), "is not some idea conjured up to boost our self-esteem but a present reality that we will enjoy in its fullness at the resurrection of the dead. At that point, we will sit on thrones alongside our Savior and enjoy by grace what is His by right."[21] (2:12a)

5) *Even when we are faithless, God remains faithful for He cannot deny Himself.* This promise immediately follows an explicit declaration that if we deny Christ, He will one day deny us before His Father at the final judgement (Mat. 10:33). This demands a distinction between denial and faithlessness. The ESV Study Bible footnote aptly explains (p. 2564, 2008 ed.), "*to deny Him must entail a more*

---

[19] See J. I. Packer, p. 170.

[20] White, R. E. O., "Sanctification." *Evangelical Dictionary of Theology,* 3rd Edition, edited by Daniel J. Treier and Walter A. Elwell, (Baker Academic, 2017), p. 1903. Adobe Digital Editions

[21] See https://www.ligonier.org/learn/devotionals/reigning-with-christ/

serious offense than being faithless. Denying Christ envisions final apostacy in contrast with a temporary lapse (faithlessness) in trusting Christ." Whereas denial involves utter repudiation of the truths about Jesus, faithlessness is momentary and not habitual. But when we are faithless, we have the absolute certainty that God will be ever faithful. Why? God cannot do anything that is inconsistent or contrary to His character. As we repent of our faithless thoughts and actions, God is ever faithful to forgive and restore, to keep His forever promises to us. (2:12b-13)

Ultimately my identity is found in the fact that I am God's. I am hidden in Christ in God. (Colossians 3:3.) I belong to Him and in Him, and through Him we are more than conquerors. As Rend Collective sings in "More than Conquerors:"

We are more than conquerors, through Christ
You have overcome this world, this life
We will not bow to sin or to shame
We are defiant in Your name
You are the fire that cannot be tamed
You are the power in our veins
Our Lord, our God, our Conqueror!

Nothing is impossible
Every chain is breakable
With You, we are victorious
You are stronger than our hearts
You are greater than the dark
With You, we are victorious[22]

---

[22] For the full song go to https://www.youtube.com/watch?v=2p8_4NbrcKA

Chapter Five
Living Out the Shame-free (Unashamed) Life in the Face of Opposition
2 Timothy 2:14-26

My early life was largely lived in what today would be called a "shame culture." Students were often corrected by being made to sit in a corner or stand in front of the class with arms outstretched, laden with books. Then there was having to stand in line in front of the school entrance, for various infractions, as the good students came in from recess. (Why was I made to do this when I had only tried, and half-way succeeded, in climbing the flagpole.) Further, it was not uncommon for a boss to publicly berate an employee or even to find one's own failings become the illustration in a Sunday sermon.

Today, shaming has taken on an even more malevolent dimension. Lies, character assassination, ostracization, hatemongering, and death threats are almost to be expected in our contemporary political climate. *So, do we Christians mimic the behavior of our opponents, certainly some do. Or do we do something different. If so, why, and how?*

As we begin, it is important to note that biblical Christians do not see themselves as having two separate lives – a "church life" and a "societal life." We live all of life, whether public or private - religious or secular - by the same scripture-based principles. When persecuted, shamed in any sphere, we turn to the holy tried and proven Word of God. There we are reminded of the words of Jesus in the Sermon on the Mount, "Blessed are you when others revile you and persecute you and utter all kinds of evil against you falsely on my account, Rejoice and be glad, for your reward is great in heaven. (Mat. 5:11-12a) When tempted to go "toe to toe," or retort with stinging words and sharp vitriol, we are reminded of the words of this passage. Yes, we find no easy answers here, but Paul does give us some *helpful guidelines* in dealing with our opponents, both inside and outside the church:

1. Stop engaging in useless, senseless quarrels (verbal battles) over mere words (2:14). Paul is referring to splitting hairs over matters of little consequence, provoking meaningless, "never ending" verbal squabbles. Why? First, the focus is all about winning or demolishing the argument of your opponent rather than a positive impact on the listeners. Meaningless quibbling over words is a waste of their time and your time. Further, it is dangerous in that it can bring ruin or extensive damage to the faith (or non-faith) of the listeners. This is especially true when one undermines, or causes confusion concerning fundamental gospel truths or gospel living. It does us well to think first, then speak or not speak at all. (*It must be noted that Paul is not saying that we cannot make a strong argument, a reasoned apologetic when important Scriptural teaching or the gospel itself is under attack. Nor is he saying that one should not engage in vital word or theological studies concerning such truths as salvation, justification, sanctification, repentance, etc.)

2. Be zealously eager to accurately interpret (and rightly behave) in line with the gospel[23] *(2:15).* One day our life and our teaching will undergo the scrutiny of God. What will that divine inspection reveal? Will we be ashamed? We will not if we engage in the hard work and rigor that is demanded to properly understand, interpret, and declare the guiding truths of Scripture. Nor will our message be thwarted by a behavior that militates against what we say we believe. People, especially your opponents, will not respect your arguments or teaching, no matter how elegantly delivered, if they cannot respect your person. The

---

[23] See Mounce, p.1078.

"straightness," authenticity and truthfulness of your speech will stand in sharp contrast to the "inadequate, arcane, and deceptive formulations" of your opponents.[24]

Peter Adam gives examples of how we can handle/interpret inaccurately biblical texts in his book, *Speaking God's Words:*[25] 1) Scripture is often lifted out of context and consequently misapplied. 2) Sometimes a text is errantly viewed through the teacher's favorite psychological, political, and/or social lens. The result is that his favorite subtext is being read into the passage. 3) A text can be moralized or organized into a list of "proof texts" to fit ones doctrinal or theological preferences. 4) And some even proport to know what the Scripture is silent about, does not address, such as Christ's teenage years. They conjecture feelings and actions taken for which they have no factual basis.' Indeed, it takes hard work to "get it right." William Willimon rightly cautions that current preaching sometimes reduces "salvation to self-esteem, sin to maladjustment, church to group therapy, and Jesus to Dear Abby."[26] There is certainly a place when applying Scripture for these other disciplines, but we must not allow ourselves to read into the biblical text what is not there. Certainly, since the Scriptures are our guidebook ("life-book") for living and interaction with others at home, at work, at church, and the larger society.

3. Avoid being pulled into contentious, bellicose, irreverent argumentation. (2:16-18) Hughes describes this godless trivial chatter as "clever,

---

[24] Towner, Philip H, "The Letters to Timothy and Titus", *The New International Commentary*, (Grand Rapids, Michigan: William B. Eerdmans Publishing Company, 2006) p.10723. Kindle.

[25] Adam, Peter, *Speaking God's Words* (Leicester, England: InterVarsity, 1996), pp.102-103.

[26] Willimon, William H, "Been There Preached That," *Leadership Magazine,* Fall 1995, p. 76.

speculative, intellectually reckless, and spiritually destructive talk."[27] It also seems to be pointed directly at basic gospel teaching. These unholy speculations make a big noise, but there is no substance behind them. Jesus warns us "not to throw your pearls before pigs, lest they trample them underfoot and turn to attack you" (Matt. 7:6). Our kingdom message is of great value and demands that we not continually, indefinitely proclaim or debate the gospel message with those who are adamant, irreverent, and hostile in their rejection of it.

Two reasons are given for our avoidance. First, what these false teachers often refer to as advancement or progress (an upward mobility) in one's life, religion, or Christianity, is in fact a devolution – an ever downward spiral deeper and deeper into the pit of ungodliness. Second, like a malignant cancer, COVID 19, this "gangrene" quickly spreads spiritual sickness throughout the church and on into society. Therefore, we must avoid what would be a futile debate with these profane proponents of a gospel which is quite foreign to the true gospel of God. *Once again, Paul does not discourage healthy debate, "nor is this a call for isolationism, but wisdom calls for avoidance of fruitless discussion that only produces envy and strife."[28]

Paul gives two false teachers as examples, Hymenaeus and Philetus who have "swerved from the truth."[29] Further, they were upsetting, if not overturning the faith of some. They were proclaiming that the final resurrection had already occurred as a spiritual resurrection, thus denying the bodily resurrection of believers. Since the believer's bodily resurrection is inseparably linked to the bodily resurrection of Christ, to deny the first would be to also deny the latter. (See I Cor. 15:12-14). At the very heart of the gospel is the death, burial, and bodily resurrection of

---

[27] Hughes, R. Kent, "1-2 Timothy and Titus," *Preaching the Word* (Wheaton, Illinois: Crossway, 2012), p. 3797 Kindle.

[28] Mounce, p. 1081.

[29] Hymenaeus had already been put under church discipline by Paul for blaspheming (I Timothy 1:20). Philetus is mentioned only here.

Christ. To deny any of this is to deny its truth, and the very essence of its message.

4. Remember, no matter how compelling or successful your opponent may seem, ultimately God will preserve, protect, and make holy His people (2:19). As you look around, it may seem like the enemies of the gospel and traditional Judeo-Christion values are winning, even within the walls of Christ's church. But they cannot and will not. Why?

Referencing Isaiah 28:16, Paul paints a picture of a building, meaning the church or elect, built by God on the firm foundation, Jesus Christ (See I Pet. 2:6). This solid foundation is unassailable and unmovable. Further, there is a two-part inscription on its cornerstone identifying, authenticating God as the builder with the words, "The Lord knows those who are His", and "Let everyone who names the name of the Lord depart from iniquity" (2:19).

The first inscription quotes the Septuagint reading of Numbers 16:5. Just as two false teachers, in Second Timothy, were rebelling against the authority of one of God's apostles, so had Korah and his followers rebelled against God's leader Moses, leading to their destruction. If God, out of the millions of Israelites, was able to discern who was against Him and afflict just punishment, He certainly can discern who are true authentic believers today and protect and preserve His church. And He can and will vindicate His followers by punishing their enemies either now or at the final judgment. We need not fear. "When the ultimate judgment fires fall in the eschaton, and the cosmos is but a cinder, the Lord will know who are His."[30]

The second inscription parallels Moses' admonition in the Korah story (Num. 16:26-27) in calling Timothy and the faithful "to dissociate themselves completely from their opponents and their teachings."[31] As fully devoted followers of Christ, we prove the authenticity of our

---

[30] Hughes, p. 3844.

[31] Towner, Philip H, p. 10982.

faith by rejecting both false teaching and the immoral lifestyle that often characterizes false teachers.

5. Live an honorable, holy life (2:20-26). Chicago Sun Times columnist Sydney J. Harris argues "Since most of us would rather be admired for what we do, rather than for what we are, we are normally willing to sacrifice character for conduct, and integrity for achievement...But when all is considered, the closer a job gets to the moral core of a person, the more important character becomes."[32] Certainly, we would want upright living in our pastors, teachers, and counselors. And whether they admit it or not, others and certainly your opponents — as hypocritical as it may be — will require it of you. Indeed, our Lord requires it of you. We will flesh out this directive using first a metaphor, explaining its meaning, and then the consequent life behaviors.

We have all marveled at great houses, such as the Biltmore or Chatsworth. Inside of them we find gilded ceilings, bright silver cutlery, fine china, the finest of paintings, furniture, tapestries, and so much more for noble use. But we also find privy closets, chamber pots, and vessels to handle ash and garbage for mundane use. Obviously, some of these vessels are displayed publicly because they bring honor and prestige to the master of the house. Others are hidden away, out of sight.

Paul uses this analogy for the visible, professing church. Within the worldwide community professing to be Christian, there are two types of teachers (as we have just seen): those honorable teachers who are true or faithful to the gospel (Paul, Timothy) and those who are dishonorable, "bogus," charlatans, teaching a false gospel of doctrinal and moral error (Hymenaeus, Philetus).[33] Early church father Chrysostom said: "Let it

---

[32] Hughes, p. 3880.

[33] Stott, p.72, Constable, 36, Earle, p.404.

not disturb thee that there are corrupt and wicked men (in the church) for in a great house there are such vessals."[34]

What follows is Paul's desire to rid the church of false teaching and false teachers. These dishonorable teachers, like toilets and drains, Paul sees as disgusting filth. Certainly, no one would want to be lumped in with them or fellowship with them. On the contrary, one can be of noble use by the Master of the house as they pursue (dedicate themselves to) an ongoing spiritual transformation meaning, cleansing themselves thoroughly of all false teaching and immoral conduct.[35] The result of this transformation is that they are made ready for ministry both inside and outside of the church.

So, specifically, what does a holy, mature Christian life look like? (see verses 22-26) *First,* we must flee (run from) the negative passions often characteristic of youth. As we watch the news, we see that youth often fall prey to impatience, wanting things quickly, immediately — right now! There is a desire to tear down long-standing societal norms and traditions at once, with no regard for the consequences. As Hughes remarks, "Today's impatience is fed by the media's quick fix. After all, on television everything gets resolved in the space of an hour."[36] Another is their headstrong obstinacy with no willingness to "hear or tolerate another viewpoint." This is combined with a mean-spirited, arrogant retort, sometimes accompanied by violence. That is why it is refreshing when youth, like Timothy, flee these vices and pursue, instead, godly virtues.

---

[34] Oden, Thomas C, "First and Second Timothy and Titus" *Interpretation: A Biblical Commentary for Teaching and Preaching* (Louisville: John Knox Press, 1981), p. 71. Adobe Digital Editions.

[35] Montague, George T, "First and Second Timothy, Titus," *Catholic Commentary on Sacred Scripture* (Grand Rapids, Michigan: Baker Academic, 2008), p. 195 Adobe Digital Editions.

[36] Hughes, p. 3925.

Second, we are to pursue (run to) the virtues of righteousness, faith, love, peace, and purity. In this list we see behavior characterized by both an upward look toward God and an outward look toward others around us, specifically here, the community of faith. Our lives should be characterized by moral excellence in conduct, a sincere trust in God and faithfulness toward others, a deep and devoted godly affection demonstrated by loyalty and compassion for others, a peacemaker mentality that shuns strife and verbal battles, and a sincere purity of heart that resists hypocrisy.[37]

Third, shun using the tactics of your opponents. Specifically, reject foolish, ignorant, controversies that breed quarrels. Towner describes them as frivolous, uneducated verbal wrangling that leads to nothing useful — destructive education rather than constructive education.[38]

Fourth, act positively toward your opponents: 1) Be kind/gentle to everyone. As in I Thess. 2:7, "But we were gentle among you, like a nursing mother taking care of her own children." Sadly, in our culture, gentleness is seen more as a vice than a virtue. It is the character of those who are spineless doormats, those who are weak, whimpering fools. But that is not how Scripture would describe it. Gentleness is meekness, but not weakness. It is controlled strength. Indeed, those who come to the omnipotent Christ find that He is a gentle Savior who gives rest to the weary and strength to the weak (Matt. 11:28-30). 2) Be a skillful teacher, both in ability and willingness to gently confront heretics. Your goal will ever be to correct error and rescue those who have fallen into error. 3) Be patient in enduring evil. We must endure evil without a spirit of resentment, bitterness, brashness, rudeness — especially when the insults fly. We must forbear when our views are

---

[37] See D. Edmond Hiebert, "Second Timothy," *Everyman's Bible Commentary* (Chicago: Moody Bible Institute, 1958), p. 1057 Kindle.

[38] Towner, p. 11149.

deliberately misrepresented and manipulated by the misinformed. 4) be humble and gentle while correcting error.

Why? It may just be that God will perform the miracle of bringing these "hard cases" to their senses, opening their minds to the truth, and turning their hearts toward God in repentance to receiving the true gospel. They who once were enslaved by the devil, so that they could not, would not understand the truth. They who stumbled about intoxicated by the Devil's lies, now are liberated from the moral and intellectual darkness of sin to a renewed sound mind. "The church never loses hope for heaven is peopled with untold numbers of Magdalens and Augustines."[39]

Mr. Dascanio was a testy, feisty, fiery sort, always looking for a verbal duel. So, as we moved into the country parsonage next door, I was given ample warning to stay clear of him. After all, he was well known for squashing fights in his bar with bat in hand, and he didn't take kindly to preachers.

I would heed the warnings for a while. Then came the day when I braved the huge, menacing German shepherd patrolling the front yard and knocked on his door. This would be the first of many to follow. He was an avid gardener who loved to brag on his prize tomatoes, peppers, beans, and potatoes. I would just sit there, ask questions, and listen. Then I accepted his invitation to grow my own garden alongside his and was given many invaluable pointers passed down from his homeland. We were becoming friends.

At times, I would sit while enduring his blistering assault on Christians, ending with questions not intended to be answered. Yet calmly, gently I would answer with the gospel woven throughout. I refused to be ashamed of my Lord. He would stop, listen, and then move on to politics. But he was listening!

---

[39] Montague, p. 199.

Mr. Dascanio was not a false teacher, though he had swallowed the lies of some false teachers. Yet God was softening his heart, and he slowly began to tell me about how he would listen every time a Billy Graham Crusade came on. Later, it became apparent that he had come to believe the gospel message. And when the day came for me to resign my parish and go to seminary, for the first time, I saw his eyes flooded with tears as he expressed the deepest affection. What he had shamed, he now accepted without shame.

Chapter Six
Shameful People and Their Shameful Acts
2 Timothy 3:1-9

Paul is about to describe, in chilling detail, false teachers who are "pernicious in their character," are of a "perverse nature," "religious pretenders, representative of the quacks and mythomaniacs of the ancient world."[40] These shameful people will characterize the "last days - a time of "moral decadence" and "moral decay."[41] *Certainly that describes the days in which we live.* Have you not heard people deploring the present hour as "difficult" (NASB, ESV), "full of danger" (Phillips), surprisingly "terrible" (NIV), a time filled with "stress" (RSV)? (See 3:1)

The present days are made terrible and stressful not only by natural disasters, open political warfare, poverty, and famine, but by the abusive evil of false teachers. This sounds serious. Well, if they are so deceptive, how then do we know if a person is a false teacher? *Their pretense, Paul unmasks with a telling, damning, vice list (2-5a):*

1. They are "lovers of self."

These people are self-centered, self-absorbed, self-worshipping, who ultimately can see no one else but themselves. Even their seemingly positive expressions toward others are fueled by self-interest and

---

[40] Lea, p. 230.

[41] Mounce, p.1110., I see the "last days" as including the time-period inaugurated by Christ's ascension, the coming of the Holy Spirit, and culminating in his Second Coming. (Heb. 1:2; Acts 2:17, Mat. 24).

self-exaltation — what lies in it for them. "The false teachers are a narcissistic lot. Having switched their soul's gravity from God to themselves, they in effect wrap their arms around themselves in loving embrace."[42]

2. *They are "lovers of money."*

Money often brings power, prestige, and the possessions they so earnestly seek. This love for money becomes the "root of all kinds of evils" (1 Tim. 6:10 ESV) of which perhaps the first is the excessive greed of avarice. Look around, an unhealthy love for money leads people to envy, jealousy, hate, theft, embezzlement, excessively low wages for employees, high prices for products, and even murder.

3. *They are" proud" and "arrogant."*

False teachers are notoriously proud and arrogant ("full of big words," Phillips). They are consumed with "prideful *thoughts*" and there is no end to their "arrogant (boastful) *words*."[43] These are people with a lofty, elitist attitude who see others as inferior in both intelligence and speech.

4. *They are "abusive."*

Scornful verbal insults, afflicted upon others, have become the norm of their day, and secondarily blasphemy directed towards God. In this they reflect the Devil, who accuses the saints, day-and-night, before the throne of God (Rev. 12:10).

5. *They are "disobedient to parents."*

First Timothy 1:9 speaks of those who stoop to striking their parents. Today it is not uncommon for children to chronically disobey and verbally or physically abuse parents. Sadly, as Hughes writes, "These false teachers would have found soul-mates today in many who write sit-com

---

[42] Hughes, p. 4026.

[43] Bernard, J. H., "The Pastoral Epistles," (Grand Rapids, Michigan: Baker, 1980), p. 130.

family comedies in which the parents are buffoons and the children are insolent savants."[44]

6. They are "ungrateful."

These teachers should have been humbled and grateful for the parents' intellect, verbal gifts, common necessities, and church family that God has provided for them. But they are wholly unappreciative.

7. They are "unholy."

They have devolved to the point where they see nothing as sacred except for their self-worship. Consequently, they have no relationship with God and adopt the unbelieving lifestyle of the world around them.

8. They are "heartless."

These people are devoid of the most basic natural affection, compassion or regard that is found between family members. They are without heart. Lea writes that these "evildoers have become almost beastlike in the breakdown of love for their kin."[45]

9. They are "unappeasable."

These people are caught up in endless feuds, since once you have offended them, there is no desire to reconcile, to forgive, or to make amends.

10. They are "slanderous."

False teachers are malicious maligners who delight in destroying the reputations of innocent people.[46]

---

[44] Bernard, J. H., "The Pastoral Epistles," (Grand Rapids, Michigan: Baker, 1980), p.130.

[45] Lea, p. 232., See also Hiebert., p.1169., Stott, p. 85.

[46] Towner, p. 11370.

11. They are "without self-control."

They are weak, unable to confront or resist temptation or to control sinful passions.

12. They are "brutal."

These savage brutes resemble fierce, untamed animals in their attitudes and actions.[47]

13. They are known for "not loving good."

The desire or appreciation for doing the right thing, the good thing, is utterly foreign to them. Virtuous living is not only unappealing, but they also despise those who pursue it.

14. They are "treacherous."

They are traitors who betray the Gospel they once claimed to espouse. Having broken faith, they now join hands with the opponents of the Christian faith.[48]

15. They are "reckless."

They foolishly "dive in, "forge ahead" with little or no forethought given to their pernicious deeds.[49]

16. They are "swollen with conceit."

Having fallen to their ongoing delusion of elevated self-importance and self-worship, they, like Oscar Wilde can say, "I have nothing to declare but my own genius."[50]

---

[47] Lea, p. 232, Mounce, p. 1116. Earle, p. 407.

[48] Towner, p. 11388.

[49] Hiebert, p. 1185

[50] Hughes, p. 4053-4.

17. They are "lovers of pleasure rather than lovers of God."

They are drunken with an insatiable desire to pursue pleasure. Since they are self-absorbed, self-serving, self-worshiping, there is no room for the antithetical behavior to that of loving or serving God.

18. They are described as *"having the appearance of godliness but denying its power."*

Paul brings to conclusion his vice list with this "stinging summary description" of the hypocrisy of these false teachers.[51] For one thing, "looking Christian", "talking Christian", being well versed in "Christian trivia"," does not, in and of itself, substantiate that you are Christian. You may engage regularly in fasting, keeping "the rules" (See 1 Timothy 1:4; 4:3), and attending church, but where is the power of spiritual trans-formation by the Holy Spirit? When you come to really know Christ, the Holy Spirit takes residence in you — producing holy living, Spirit-fruit, and the exchange of self-love for the love and worship of God, and God alone.

The apostasy by these leaders, these supposedly spiritual teachers, can only elicit one valid response. You must "avoid such people" (3:5b). The ESV Study Bible — note (3:5, p. 2565) suggests that the avoidance may demand excommunication — exclusion from the Christian fellow-ship (church) — when the apostate stubbornly refuses to repent and turn away from their error.

One might react by asking, "Why?" Does this not seem a little harsh? Paul responds, giving three reasons:

1. Like the beasts that they are, these "religious sneaks" creep into households using "stealth tactics."[52] (6-7)

---

[51] Mounce, p. 1116.

[52] See Hughes, p. 4082, Fee, p. 271.

As we have seen, false teachers are especially dangerous to the church, due to their deception. Here, they "worm their way" (NIV) into wealthy "house-churches" targeting a specific group of women (certainly not women in general) characterized as:

1) "weak" ("silly women," NRSV; "vulnerable," NLT)

2) "burdened with sins," meaning these past/present sins have piled up, inflicting a heavy psychological and spiritual load of guilt.

3) unable to defend against various sinful impulses and enslaving "sinful passions."

4) "always learning and never able to arrive at the knowledge of the truth." These incessant learners go through a fruitless "cycle of instruction in senseless myths, and quibbling about words, followed by payment leading to more senseless babble."[53] In all of it, they come no closer to the freedom from guilt and destructive sinful habits, which they could have found in true repentance and saving faith in the good news of the gospel message.

2. The message and lifestyle of false teachers is in direct opposition to the gospel truth (8).

Paul uses Jannes and Jambres as examples of those who oppose the truth. Their names, as the Egyptian magicians who were Moses' arch nemeses (Exod. 7:8-13), would have been well-known to Timothy.[54] These, like today's false teachers are "corrupted in mind and disqualified regarding the faith." Why, because their depraved minds have neither the moral nor intellectual capacity to comprehend the truth. Do you really want them teaching adult education or sitting on your governing board? No, they are useless, incapable of either grasping the gospel faith or living it out. Further, their message and morals have been tested and

---

[53] Mounce, p. 1120.

[54] See Towner for a great discussion on these men, pp. 11485 ff.

are found wanting. They will never measure up to God's standards for leadership (See 1 Tim. 3; Titus 1).

3. They "will not get very far." (9)

They may appear to be unstoppable now, but they will meet their doom. There comes a time when their error is exposed for what it is. That is just the news that Timothy and we need to hear. Jesus is going to win. For the Christian, the best is always yet to come.

Before we move on, Ligonier's State of Theology Survey 2018[55] gives us pause in that it demonstrates how little theology many people know, and how "Christians" today, at times, unknowingly hold fast to forms of error. A few examples:

1) Seventy-eight per-cent agreed that "Jesus is the first and greatest being *created* by God" (the Arian heresy). No, Jesus is fully God and is not a created being (John 1:1-3, 14).

2) Fifty-three per-cent of those 18-34 believed that the Bible is not literally true, whereas Jesus said, "Thy word is truth" (John 17:17).

3) Fifty-one per-cent of those age 18-34, believed that "the Bible's condemnation of homosexuality does not apply to today. Jesus makes it clear in Matthew 5:17-18 that the moral law code has not been abrogated.

4) Fifty-one per-cent of Evangelicals believe that God accepts the worship of all religions. Jesus, in John 4:24 and 14:6, makes it clear that Christ is the only way to heaven and that true worship must be centered in and on Christ alone.

---

[55] The survey is found at https://thestateoftheology.com/.

The Christian Post reports more recently, "Americans losing grip on most basic tenets of Christian faith:"[56]

1) They cite a recent George Barna survey in which only fifty-one percent of Americans consider God to be "all-powerful, all-knowing, perfect and just creator of the universe who still rules the world today." Nearly half were not convinced that God exists.

2) They note that the latest research from the twelve-part American Worldview Inventory also documents that only forty-one percent held the biblical perspective that Christ lived a sinless life and was both fully man and fully God.

3) "Over half of all adults — fifty-two percent — contend that 'the Holy Spirit is not a living entity, but merely a symbol of God's power, presence or purity."

4) In the report, Barna noted to the Christian Post, "We've transitioned from a people who upheld the existence of absolute moral truth to a nation that rejects moral absolutes. The result has been a seminal shift in our collective focus, from other to self, and from absolute truths to conditional truths. That helps to explain why the 'doesn't/don't know/don't care' population, regarding the existence of God, has mushroomed from 8 percent to 32 percent in just 30 years,"

5) Barna further adds, "The spiritual noise in our culture over the last few decades has confused and misled hundreds of millions of people. The message to churches, Christian leaders, and Christian educators is clear: we can no longer assume that people have a solid grasp of even the most basic biblical principles."

---

[56] The April 25, 2020 article by Brandon Showalter can be found at: https://www.christianpost.com/news/americans-losing-grip-on-most-basic-tenets-of-christian-faith-survey.html

These few examples show how important the study of the Bible and theology are if we are to both recognize and refute false teaching. We too have our work cut out for us in this area. No wonder then, that one of the first things apostates will tell you is that you don't need to study doctrine.

Chapter Seven
Encouragement on How to Stand in the Face of Fierce Opposition
2 Timothy 3:10-17

I have often responded to the question, "How are you doing?" by simply saying, "I'm pressing on." Indeed, in view of the picture Paul has painted of the opposition, we too may be struggling with how to "keep going," how to continue "pressing on." Once again, Paul comes to the rescue by encouraging us with the good news that we can survive if we, *1) follow his example, and 2) as we are daily energized and equipped by the life-giving, life-preserving Sacred Scriptures.* We can avoid the vices of these apostates and, in sharp contrast, exemplify the virtues of a committed follower of Christ.

I. The Example of Paul (3:10-13):

Paul begins with the Spirit-empowered virtues exemplified in the disciplined, Christ-following life. "Look at me", Paul says, "imitate what you see; do as I do!" "Be imitators of me as I am of Christ (1 Cor. 11:1)." We all need mentors. Paul had been that mentor. Yes, Timothy had investigated, "traced out," taken special note of Paul's manner of life,[57] now he must own it, and to some degree, replicate it. Paul is emphatic and personal as he delineates a virtue list with the repetitive use of "my" eight times (my teaching, my conduct, ... *3:10-11*).

---

[57] Lea, p. 238

Nine nouns form a composite picture of virtuous living. They are Paul's:

1. "Teaching" — the glorious gospel message centered on and around the death, burial, and resurrection of Christ (1 Cor. 15:1-3). We would add the Pauline doctrines of the righteousness of God, sin, the law, salvation by grace through faith, forgiveness, adoption, justification, sanctification, the body of Christ/the church, the doctrine of the kingdom, baptism, the Lord's Supper, the doctrine of the Holy Spirit, Christian liberty, the resurrection, and glorification... (See the Pauline Epistles.) All believers should be committed to understanding these great doctrines.[58] They tell us what to believe, how to behave, and give us the essential truths of the faith against which all other teaching must be measured.

2. "Conduct" — his "way of life" (NIV) Look at the way I live, says Paul, and the principles that guide my conduct. What I teach is lived out in what I do. You won't see me saying one thing, and then doing another. My walk matches my talk! Can that be said of us?

3. "Aim in life" — Paul's resolve was to live totally committed to Christ and to fulfill his commission from Christ to be an apostle to the gentiles (Phil. 1:21; Rom. 11:13).

---

[58] Some suggestions for further study toward understanding biblical doctrine: 1) *Use a good Study Bible's articles and resources section* to see overviews of the various biblical doctrines, biblical ethics, biblical interpretation, biblical inerrancy, and the Bible contrasted with various cults and world religions (e.g. Crossway ESV Study Bible); 2) Become familiar with a good *Systematic Theology* which will give insight into the *Doctrine of the Bible, Doctrine of God, Doctrine of Man, Doctrine of Christ and the Holy Spirit, Doctrine of Salvation, Doctrine of the Church and Doctrine of the Future as well as the different Confessions of the Faith* (e.g. Grudem's Systematic Theology; Christian Theology by Millard J. Erickson; Contours of Christian Theology; Systematic Theology by Louis Berkhof; A Theology of Lordship By John Frame; Integrative Theology by Gordon Lewis and Bruce Demarest; Anglican Theology by Mark Chapman; 3) *Become familiar with a good Historical Theology* which can be defined as the study of how Christians during different historical periods have understood different theological subjects or topics (e.g. *Historical Theology* by Gregg R. Allison; *Historical Theology* by Alistair E. McGrath).

4. "Faith" — his absolute, implicit trust in God in every circumstance, even when things made no sense.

5. "Patience" — Look at the way God has enabled me in my ministry with "the ability to wait for results and to persevere in the face of opposition."[59]

6. "Love" — that unconditional, constant love toward all "taking the form of sacrificial, costly service done for others,"[60] "embracing friend and foe alike."[61]

7. "Steadfastness" — that brave patience that endures suffering.

8. "Persecutions" — those sufferings Paul experienced for sharing the gospel, for just being a Christian. Paul names three cities in Galatia where he had gone on his first missionary journey. One of them, Lystra, was Timothy's hometown. Timothy had either heard or witnessed the day when Paul was stoned, dragged out of the city, and left for dead (Acts 14:19-23). He would never forget it!

9. "Sufferings" — hardships in general. Second Corinthians 11:16-33 and the book of Acts give a gruesome account of the many sufferings of Paul, culminating in a final dungeon imprisonment (and according to tradition, his beheading).

These verses climax with an exclamation of victory, "Yet from them all the Lord rescued me." (*3:11*; See Psalm 33:20). You will never walk alone! Sometimes God will deliver (rescue) you out of and away from suffering, but always He will rescue you by walking with you, strengthening you through the suffering. Even if the persecutors take your life, they cannot win, because instantly you will be in the presence of our Lord (II Cor. 5:8).

---

[59] Towner, p. 11643.

[60] Ibid., p. 11643.

[61] Lea, p. 238. Hiebert, p. 1294.

Part of enduring suffering is to expect it. Indeed "all who live a godly life in Christ Jesus will be persecuted (3:12). We cannot avoid suffering. It will enter every facet of our lives. Therefore, to be consumed with constant anger or to be decimated by ongoing depression is not a choice that we wish to make. It simply cannot and will not help. It won't help to endlessly declare, "I don't deserve this!" Whether you do, or do not, will not make things better. But what will, is to see suffering more as a scalpel than a sword.

We "will seldom know the micro reasons for our sufferings, but the Bible does give us faith-sustaining macro reasons."[62] What then is the purpose and promise of suffering? Here are three of them: In chapter two, we gave the *first* reason: *Suffering is God's tool to allow us the privilege of sharing in the sufferings of Christ with the promise of getting to know Him even better (Phil. 3:10).*

Second, suffering is God's tool to lead us to repentance (a turning away from destructive beliefs and behaviors in humble confession) that leads to healing, restoration, obedience, and maturity. Much of our suffering is self-afflicted. We eat wrongly, speak wrongly, think wrongly, work wrongly...and then we bear the rotted fruit of our actions. But when we agree with God about the repugnance of these thoughts and actions, we receive not only full forgiveness and restored intimacy, but we are empowered to live in an obedient, prudent life-giving way that frees us from further heartaches in the future. Why? We gradually replace the destructive behaviors of anger, malice, slander, lust, obscenities, and profanities with the productive behaviors of humility, patience, honesty, self-control, purity and encouragement (Heb. 12:6-11; James 1:2-4; Gal. 5:19-23). Life's trials crush our trouble-breeding pride and replace it with a humbled mind. And with this new outlook comes new outcomes.

Third, suffering is God's tool to force you to rely on Him, which will lead not only to a life of victory here, but a glimpse, a preview, of an eternity

---

[62] See http://www.desiringgod.org/articles/five-purposes-for-suffering

of unsurpassed indescribable joy there (2 Cor. 1:8-9; 4:17). When God has removed all your props, all that gives you the smugness of self-suffi-ciency, He is now able to display unlimited power unhindered through you and in you. All our fretting over (and even the agonies of) momen-tary sufferings, when compared to an eternity without them (multiplied trillions of years and beyond), seem small, even foolish. When we look away from our problems and fix our eyes on what is coming, the new heaven and earth, we are lost in the wonder of exploring the galaxies, picnicking in the Edenic gardens, invigorating conversations with the saints of all the ages, and being held in the arms of our Creator and Savior. O what a day that will be!

In *3:13*, we come face to face with the "progress" of the opposition—"evil people and impostors will go on from bad to worse, deceiving and being deceived." These deceivers, these cheats are progressing alright—not for the better, but from bad to worse, from the plaudits of men to ultimate judgement and eternal separation from God. Why? Because they who knowingly have deceived others have, without their knowl-edge, been hoodwinked, by the greatest deceiver of all, the devil himself. The shamed will one day be the winners, the ones who shame, the losers.

II. *The Energizing, Enriching Scriptures (3:14-17)*

Lea writes, "Timothy had learned the gospel and its demands from a compassionate cadre of teachers...Timothy's need was not to search out new novelties on which he might squander his energies, but to remain in the truths he had learned."[63] Timothy had had the early oral tradition of a reliable, God-fearing grandmother and mother, as well as a spiritual mentor in Paul — they, who in-the-midst-of their various trials had not only survived but thrived, and who had demonstrated that they had a faith that could be counted on. From five years of age, they had faithfully and properly taught him the O.T. Scriptures *(3:14-15a)*.

---

[63] Lea, p. 240.

All of us who have had the joy of saving faith will forever be indebted to a host of people along the way. My Mom and Dad, both professors, one a pastor, "infected" me with their passion for knowing and living out the Scriptures and introduced me again and again to the gospel news. My elementary Sunday school teacher, Mrs. Pine, and later, Mrs. Smeal, made the Scriptures come alive as if I had been transported backward in time. In Good News Club the "wordless book, "in word and song," shared with me each week a gospel invitation; and our Bible church encouraged me to memorize 100+ verses of Scripture. At Manahath Camp and Bible to Youth Camp, I heard theologians, Bible teachers, and missionaries from all around the world open-up the Scriptures and tell their stories. All laid the groundwork for July 4, 1967, when I would fully understand and received Christ as my Savior and Lord.

O how I remember that day. Dr. Mundell had been teaching on the dry bones of Ezekiel (Chapters 36-37). Of course, the melody and lyrics "them bones, them bones, them dry bones" jumped about inside my head. But as he went on, I gave strict attention. Soon my heart would pound. I knew I too was dead inside. I wanted to live, really live! He never gave an invitation that day, but I ran down the aisle anyway. I wanted that new life, that new heart the prophet spoke about. On America's birthday, I had a birthday. I surrendered my life to Christ. Praise God, I had joined the body of the redeemed from every tongue, tribe, and nation. I was fifteen.

What I have discovered is that only the Scriptures impart true wisdom: 1) by pointing, first and foremost, to the life, death, and resurrection of the one who saves us, Christ Jesus, 2) by describing the process of how we come by faith to salvation, 3) by teaching us the progressive nature of salvation in which we are freed from the penalty of sin in justification, from the power of sin in sanctification, and in eternity from the presence of sin in glorification. How remarkably different this is from the imposters, Paul's opponents, "who are not wise (see 3:9, 13), and who teach not the sacred writings, but human commandments."[64]

In *3:16-17*, Paul lays the groundwork for the authority of the Scriptures. We will ask: who wrote it; what is meant by "all Scripture"; what is meant by God-breathed"; and how is it profitable? *(3:16-17)*

1. Who wrote it?

The answer is that God wrote it. "All Scripture is breathed out by *God*." The apostle Peter states emphatically that no prophecy of Scripture was of human origin, rather it came into existence through the Spirit's leading. The O.T. writers were "moved" or "carried along" by the Holy Spirit. (2 Peter 1:20, 21) Again, and again, the prophets would say, "Thus says the Lord." Here in Second Timothy, Paul says that all of Scripture originated in the mind of God.

2. What is meant by "all Scripture?"

Certainly, the entire Old Testament is in view here, and by implication the New Testament books (Matthew, Mark, Luke, and others) that were already written. The list, of today's twenty-seven N. T. books was later settled and universally accepted, without reservation, by 367 A. D. Therefore, we can say that Scripture includes, and is limited to, the sixty-six books of the Bible.[65]

3. What is meant by "God breathed?"

I illustrated this in my theology classes by asking the students to put their hand directly in front of their face. I would then ask them to

---

[64] Mounce, p. 1148.

[65] For an informative discussion of what books are to be included in Scripture (the Canon of Scripture), and why, see: John M. Frame, "The Doctrine of God," *A Theology of Worship*, Vol. 4. (Phillipsburg, N.J.: P&R Publishing Company, 2010), p. 2825-2956. Kindle; Wayne Grudem, *Systematic Theology: An Introduction to Biblical Doctrine* (Zondervan, Grand Rapids, Michigan, 2015), p. 62-87.

speak a few words and tell me what they discovered. The obvious answer was that they could feel their breath on their hand. My point is that Scripture is God's personal, spoken word to us. God spoke, men wrote.

Exactly what is the relationship between the God who spoke and the men who wrote? Did God simply dictate word for word the Scriptures? On rare occasions, that would be true, such as when God dictated the law to Moses (Exod. 34:27). But a close look at the human writers of Scripture shows distinct differences in the words they used, the emotions they felt, and even their mastery of the biblical languages. Most theologians, for example, John Frame, explain: "God used all the distinct personal qualities of each writer. God used the differences of heredity, environment, upbringing, education, gifts, talents, styles, interests, idiosyncrasies to reveal His word...he provides a wide variety of writers with a rich diversity of experience."[66]

But not only did God allow the full, personal humanity of each writer to be part of the words of Scripture, the Holy Spirit superintended, influenced their every word, guaranteeing an accurate record of the divine revelation.[67] Thus we join Jesus in saying, "Thy word is truth (John 17:17). "So, there is no reason to deny that (it is) God's personal words (not just thoughts) take written form in the canonical books he has given to us."[68]

4. How is Scripture "profitable"?

What Paul is saying here is that Scripture is sufficient, totally adequate, forever useful. "For what, you ask." Grudem explains: Scripture "contains everything we need for God to tell us for salvation, for trusting

---

[66] Frame, 3005.

[67] Erickson, Millard, *Christian Theology*, (Baker Academic: Grand Rapids, Michigan, 2013), p. 178. Adobe Digital Editions.

[68] Frame, p. 3037.

Him perfectly, and for obeying Him perfectly."[69] Paul makes his point by declaring that when Scripture's work on you is done, you will be made "complete, equipped for every good work." You will be fully outfitted to live the Christian life and to stand tall and strong in the face of any opposition — intellectually, morally, relationally, and spiritually. Everything you need is found in Scripture.

Paul points to four ways in which the Scriptures are found useful to pastors and parishioners alike:

1) For teaching — The Bible is the source, the solid foundation for all doctrinal and theological instruction. That is why it is imperative that we study and read faithfully from all parts and genres of Scripture. Frame admonishes, "All Scripture is breathed out by God, not just those parts we find attractive, cogent, relevant, or culturally respectable."[70] Many a false doctrine originates from tunnel vision, a myopic view of Scripture.

2) For reproof — Well-rounded study of the Bible enables one to detect, reject, and rebuke doctrinal errors or falsehoods and expose personal forms of immorality.[71] This must be done in a firm yet loving spirit.

3) For correction — This differs from reproof in that it comes from the positive side and focuses on rehabilitation and restoration. The desire is to make one whole again.[72] "It straightens us out (NLT)."

4) For training in righteousness — The Bible provides the training necessary for doing what is morally right — principles and everyday illustrations of what it means to be holy.

---

[69] Grudem, p. 152.

[70] Frame, p. 3450.

[71] See Hiebert, p. 1420; Lea, p. 244; Towner, p. 11998.

[72] See Ralph Earle, "1&2 Timothy," *The Expositors Bible Commentary, Vol. 11* (Grand Rapids, Michigan: Zondervan, 1981) p. 410.

Do you have a mentor, a Christian who is strong in their faith, who is of strong character? A Christian who loves God and gets excited when you even mention the word, Bible. Do you have someone who can guide you in learning what to believe, and how to behave, who will take the time to listen, laugh, even shed tears with you and for you? If not, pray, beat on the doors of heaven, and see if God does not bring that person into your life. If you persist, He will!

Chapter Eight
The Ultimate Charge to the Unashamed
2 Timothy 4:1-8

Nearly every day now, we come face to face with the reincarnation of the Salem Witch Trials. The traditionalists are the condemned and the secularists are the trial judges. These everywhere-present inquisitors search out the traditional bigots and religious racists who are trolling the social media platforms and proclaiming their neo-gospel message across the airwaves. The tenets of this new pervasive, secularist faith declare that:

1. No dissent from the neo-progressive dogma will be tolerated.

Such dissenters will be found out and stamped out. They will be targeted at their workplaces, in and outside of their homes, at the stores, on the campuses, on social media, and even in the houses of Congress. And they will be brought to this newfound justice. For the safety of the country, no freedom of speech must be allowed for these traditionalists.

2. All forms of sex outside of marriage are permissible, indeed preferable.

"Doing what you want is the new master ethic...All traditional moral codes represent systems of unjust repression... Yesterday's sinners have become the new secular saints; and yesterday's sins have become virtues."[73]

---

[73] Eberstadt, p. 23.

3. Freedom of Religion in many, if not all its expressions must be eradicated from the public square.

Alastair Bruce, who was paid to ensure the historical accuracy of *Downton Abbey*, bemoaned the difficulty of producing the show without revealing, and therefore resulting in, the elimination of many religious practices common to that era such as prayers before meals and the napkins being folded in the shape suggesting a bishop's miter. Even the word "abbey" in the title was brought under scrutiny.[74]

Enter Paul and the summary charge to his co-worker, Timothy, predicting not only the present-day realities, but the coming judgement for all who practice this "new" secular gospel. By virtue of his schooling in the teachings of the faith, the divine origin of Scripture, and the examples of those who had lived it out in front of him, Timothy had been outfitted to receive and obey this charge.

I. The Grounds for this Charge (4:1)

1) The Coming Judgment of Christ Jesus

You live out your life (and whatever ministry to which you are called) under the scrutiny and gaze of two formidable, reliable, majestic witnesses. They are God the Father and His Son to whom He has handed over the Final Judgement (John 5:22) of all who are alive at His return, and those whose deaths have preceded His arrival. This is a helpful reminder when we are tempted to accommodate or do the bidding of the opposers of Christ. We do not answer to them.

2) The Coming Again of Christ Jesus

Everything we do is done in the light of Christ's return. We want to be confident and not ashamed when He parts the skies with heaven's

---

[74] Ibid, p.32.

armies. First John 2:28-29 tells us that it is remaining obedient to the truth of Scripture that expels and prevents that shame.

3) The Culmination of the Kingdom in Christ Jesus

There is coming a glorious day when the entire universe and its inhabitants will be subjugated to the eternal reign of Christ (Dan. 7:14; Rev. 11:15). Gone will be sin, death, Satan, and the teachers of this false, destructive, and damning gospel.

II. The Charge Itself (4:2)

Five imperative verbs demonstrate a no-nonsense militaristic approach! As Kent Hughes remarks, "The abruptness of these commands conveys urgency, terminal urgency. Timothy must waste no time. He must get to it!"[75] Paul clearly understands Timothy's, and our propensity, to put off those things that run contrary to our particular disposition.

1) "Preach the word."

Now, some of you are saying "I am not a preacher," and are ready to move on. Yes, this is primarily directed at pastors, but all of us are to share the truths of the gospel with others whether they be our neighbors, our relatives, our children, or our small group. This gospel is the core message of the entire Scriptures, not just a tool of evangelism.

We are to proclaim the truth of God's Word with the enthusiasm of the town-crier of yesteryear. Every God-given opportunity to share the "good news" brings with it the possibility of the listener being delivered from the kingdom of darkness into the kingdom of God's Son. We are all part of a worldwide mission to bring as many as we are enabled to into the kingdom.

---

[75] Hughes, p. 4441.

2) "Be ready in season and out of season."

Always be ready whatever the circumstance. So "be prepared when it is opportune or inopportune."[76] Like many others, when I have felt like the time was not convenient or I was not up to the task, that is when God did His greatest work in me and through me.

3) "Reprove"

Here the emphasis is on using arguments to reveal, create awareness of the error or sin that has captured or is tormenting the listener.[77] The purpose is to allow them to acknowledge it for what it is.

4) "Rebuke"

Paul now follows with a stronger word that focuses on confrontation. It involves one being openly, if not publicly challenged or warned, as you would a false teacher or a habitual unrepentant sinner.[78]

5) "Exhort"

We are to encourage or comfort the faint of heart or others haunted by fears of oppression or the belief that they have no chance of God's forgiveness, etc.[79]

Paul concludes the verse by saying that the exhortation must be done with great patience and careful instruction.[80] Although there is an urgency, we must not force a response, but be ever mindful that just as it took time with us, it will take time for others. We are simply to obey and allow the Holy Spirit to do the work.

---

[76] Mounce, p. 1161.

[77] Towner, p. 12215; Lea, p. 250; Stott, p. 108.

[78] Towner, p. 12225; Fee, p. 285.

[79] Earle, p. 411; Stott, p. 108.

[80] Towner, p. 12225.

Billy Graham was once asked why one of his converts was doing... a litany of sins. Quietly he said, "That is the problem, it was one of *my* converts."

III. The Reasons for the Charge (4:3-4)

Difficult and dark days are coming soon when Timothy (as well as us today) will find members of the church engaging in four destructive behaviors:

1) They "will not endure sound teaching."

They will not tolerate and therefore reject sound doctrine. The teaching of Scripture will be totally unacceptable to them, and they will "seek to stamp it out."[81] It seems that the response of rejection will not just be toward the message, but toward the messenger himself.[82]

2) "They will accumulate for themselves teachers to suit their own passions."

Ever sense the days of Timothy, these "last days" have been characterized by people amassing a whole cadre of teachers who tickle their ears, telling them what they want to hear, instead of what they need to hear. Only teachers who will condone and legitimize their sinful lusts or satisfy their cravings for the latest fashionable ideas of so-called scholars, will meet their approval. Theirs is a wanderlust for the unfamiliar ramblings and the unbeaten moral path.[83]

3) They "turn away from listening to the truth."

They make a conscious choice to forsake the truth of the Scriptures and to believe the lie of their teachers.

---

[81] Oden, p. 137.

[82] Marshall, I. H., "the Pastoral Epistles," *International Critical Commentary*, (T&T Clark International: London, 2006), p. 802.

[83] Lea, p. 252.

4) They "wander off into myths."

As Hughes laments, "Whole intellectual careers (today) are made and spent on demythologizing the Bible and reducing the words of Jesus to a few moralizing soundbites."[84] Demythologizing the Bible is the attempt to make the Bible acceptable and relevant by removing the supernatural. The result is that all the miracles are removed (e.g., virgin birth; water into wine, the resurrection, etc.), anything that cannot be explained by science. It naturally follows that there is no God who created the universe. Christ is only a human. In effect, our faith, if understood in this way, "goes up in smoke."

IV. The Charge to Timothy 4:5

In the light of what he has just heard, it would make sense if Timothy were to throw his hands up in the air, to give up and shut up. But Paul quickly adds four more imperatives meant to be rehearsed again and again in the face of trouble and opposition. I know this will be tough so:

1) "Keep your head in all situations." (NIV)

When others mindlessly race off to follow the latest religious fad and gospel "innovation," you be clearheaded, alert to the danger of these deceiving doctrines. Be composed in both speech and action. As Stott remarks, "When men and women get intoxicated with heady heresies and sparkling novelties, ministers must keep calm and sane."[85]

2) "Endure suffering,"

You will suffer ill treatment and hardship, but you must stand strong, refusing to compromise, to give even an inch. Suffering is the constant companion of a minister of the gospel.

---

[84] Hughes, p. 4513

[85] Stott, p. 112.

3) "Do the work of an evangelist."

Timothy is to spend his life in making the gospel known both inside and outside the church. Christ in His perfect life, death, burial, and resurrection has dealt a mortal blow to Satan. Therefore, all have the opportunity to be forever delivered from the penalty, power, and presence of sin. Now that is the best of news!

4) "Fulfill your ministry."

Timothy must be faithful in discharging all his duties, staying at it until the job is done. As Lea and Hiebert remark, the term for ministry is a general one referring to all acts of service for the Lord, not a term exclusive to pastoral ministry.[86]

The fulfilling of these imperatives is most urgent in the light of Paul's impending departure from this life. They serve as an introduction to 4:6-8 drawing "a contrast between Timothy, still in the thick of the fight, and Paul who has fought the grand fight."[87]

Parting Thoughts (4:6-8)

As Paul sits in the dungeon awaiting his execution, He faces death without fear and without shame. Yes, how different is the death of those who have been freed from their shame by the gospel of Christ. In the words of Frederick Langbridge, "Two men looked through the bars. One saw the mud, the other, the stars.[88]

Two vivid images describe the imminence of Paul's parting (4:6). The first is the pouring out of wine at the base of the altar as part of the O.T. ritual sacrifice (Exod. 29:40-41). *Paul could be using this wine

---

[86] Lea, p. 252; Hiebert, p. 1516.

[87] Hendriksen, W, "Exposition of the Pastoral Epistles," *New Testament Commentary,* (Baker: Grand Rapids, Michigan, 1965.) p. 287.

[88] Langbridge, Frederick, *A Cluster of Quiet Thoughts,* (London: The Religious Tract Society, 1886), n.p.

imagery as picturing his own blood being poured out at his impending death. Indeed, from the moment of his conversion his entire life had been a "living sacrifice." He had given God his everything — "his possessions, his body, his brilliant mind, his passions, his position, his reputation, his relationships, his dreams."[89] And now, the pouring out that began at conversion would climax in the departure of his soul. There would be nothing left to give as he entered the presence of his Lord.

Second, the word "departure" was used in Greek literature to describe the untying of a boat by loosening it from its moorings or the striking of the tent in preparation for a march (in Paul's case, down the Appian Way). His ship has lifted its anchor, and his final voyage has begun.

As life ebbs away, Paul can boldly declare, "I have fought the good fight, I have finished the race, I have kept the faith." (4:7). His life has been a living fulfillment of his proclamation, "I am not ashamed" (1:12). Paul was the consummate warrior,[90] standing fearlessly toe to toe with the enemy of our soul, Satan, and his ambassadors. He had relentlessly engaged in a "good" fight for the gospel. And in so doing, "he had been running in the noblest, grandest run of them all."[91]

He had finished his course. His singular desire had been to finish well. And by well, he meant to complete the ministry, the course that Christ had commissioned him to do — going everywhere, testifying to the good news of God's grace in salvation. (Acts 20:24).

He had kept the faith. It is difficult to know exactly what Paul means by "the faith." But in the broad context of the book, it seems likely that

---

[89] Hughes, p. 4574.

[90] See R. Kent Hughes, *Ephesians: The Mystery of the Body of Christ* (Wheaton, Illinois: Crossway, 1990), p. 255.

[91] Fee, p. 289.

Paul has wedded the two concepts of his own perseverance in the faith and his obligation to protect the treasure of the gospel truth from error.[92]

Paul will now receive his just reward. On the final day of judgment, the Lord will give a crown of righteousness to Paul, and to all believers, who have faithfully run the race. These are they whose righteous actions have demonstrated their love for God, and who have an insatiable longing for his appearing. And as they receive their reward, they will do so with the full understanding that it was God who enabled this upright, holy lifestyle to be produced in them. Further, they will be blessed by the overwhelming realization that the work God began in them will be completed (Phil. 1:6). That is, their righteousness will be perfected in the eternal state where they (and all glorified believers) will live forever free from their sinful disposition, with one act of righteousness perpetually followed by another.

---

[92] Towner, p. 12447

Chapter Nine
True Friends for Tough Times
2 Timothy 4:9-18

One of the amazing realities between fellow believers is that when they find a true friend, they find an eternal friend, a friend forever. Indeed, perhaps the most beautiful part of "ending well," is to end one's life within the company of friends. It is not things that get you through the tough times, it is people! We are given a hint of the urgency of the hour in Paul's desire for Timothy to secure passage before the shipping lanes are closed for the winter (4:21). As Paul approaches death, he gives some final instructions, and begins the process of sharing his final greetings to his forever friends.

1. Timothy, please *come to me soon*! (4:9-11a, 12) Why?

1)   My former friend and travelling companion,[93] Demas, has turned out to be a *fair-weather friend*. When the going got tough, he got going. He deserted me. His apparent love for the comforts of this world led to a rejection of the "shame" and fear he and others were feeling. Had not the Doctor of the Faith been convicted of sedition and soon would lose his head? For Demas, further association with Paul could lead to nothing good. So back to his hometown Thessalonica, he goes.[94]

---

[93] See Colossians 4:14 and Philemon 24

[94] Chrysostom, PG 62.655; Mounce, p. 1193.

2) Crescens and Titus, also co-workers, have probably been sent away by Paul on missionary journeys to Galatia (modern Turkey, or possibly France or northern Italy) and Dalmatia (modern Yugoslavia). Tychicus will now become Timothy's replacement in Ephesus. They will needfully be *friends from afar*. We know nothing more about Crescens, but Titus is referred to by Paul as his "true child," (Titus 1:4)

3) Only Luke is still with Paul at Rome. Luke, Paul's biographer, had been a *constant companion* forever by his side during his missionary journeys (see the "we passages" of Acts[95]), first imprisonment (Colossians 4:14; Philemon 24), and now his final days. As his private physician, he was also there to tend his wounds and chronic illness.

2. *Get Mark and bring him with you.* (4:11b)

Mark is Paul's *reconciled friend*. Given the history of the two, it is most surprising when we read, *he is very useful to me for ministry*. Mark has moved from useless to useful. Once he was seen by Paul as a deserter on Paul's first missionary journey (Acts 13:13). So repulsive had been this incident that when Barnabas suggests including Mark later, a sharp disagreement (full-blown argument) causes the separation of these two close friends (Acts 15:36-41). It seems the healing that had at least partially occurred by Paul's first imprisonment (Col. 4:10-11) has now been fully completed. As to the exact nature of Mark's usefulness, we are not told. But perhaps it is public preaching and gospel teaching in general and/or something of a personal nature.[96]

This is good news for us! As Hughes writes, "Past failure, even rejection does not prevent present usability. You can come back from disgrace...even a shirker can become a major worker in the gospel

---

[95] Acts 20:6; 21:15; 24:23; 28:16.

[96] Lea, p. 266; Mounce, p. 1193; Towner, p. 12672; Fee, p. 294.

enterprise."[97] So often our God, in His immeasurable grace, is a God of "second chances" for those whose failure has been followed by repentance and the desire for reconciliation.

We have all experienced these various types of friends. We have been hurt and often surprised by those fair-weather friends who were with us during the good times but vanished the moment things got tough. We have expressed tears of parting when those we have led to the Lord or discipled are now gone off to another country or continent. We are humbled, relieved, cry tears of joy when a friend estranged has once again become a friend indeed. And there are those loving, loyal deep relationships with those who ever walk alongside us through thick and thin. O the gift of friends!

3. *When you come* (meaning Timothy) *bring the cloak...also the books, and above all the parchments.* (4:13)

A) The *cloak* was a large, circular, heavy garment, much like a poncho, with only a hole for the head, and was made of wool or goat hair.[98] This would provide warmth and protection for the imminent cold of winter, especially in a dark, dank dungeon.

B) The *books and parchments* cannot be defined with any specificity. The books would have been made of papyrus and the parchments of a more durable animal skin. Since the parchments would be more expensive and last longer, one can conclude (especially with the words, *above all*) that they were much more important to Paul. As to their content, we can only make an educated guess. The books probably refer to the O. T. Scriptures and the parchments to Paul's personal notes. Some postulate that the parchments may have included Paul's own writings, early Christian exegesis of the Old

---

[97] Hughes, p.4777.

[98] See Lea, p. 266; Towner, p. 12723.

Testament, Christian sermons, sayings of Jesus, or early accounts of Christ's life.[99] Bottom line, we don't know.

What we do know is that Paul is not pining away or succumbing to depression. Instead, he is pressing on to his very last breath, acquiring the resources and the team to further the gospel ministry now, and when he is gone. Around him will soon be gathered, Luke, Timothy, and Mark.

4. Beware, *be on your guard* for *Alexander the coppersmith.* (4:14-15)

1) Why? Because he had done Paul personally *much harm.* He had *strongly opposed* Paul, both in word and deed. But when and how? We have little to go on. Perhaps he was one of Paul's accusers at his first trial and/or was instrumental in his arrest and first imprisonment in Rome.[100] If this is the same man who opposed Paul in I Timothy 1:20, and was subsequently excommunicated, Alexander may still be in Ephesus and could bring harm to Timothy just as he had done to Paul. Hence the warning.

2) Regardless, we can rest assured that those who do harm to the servants of the gospel will one day receive their just due when they stand before our Lord in judgement (4:14; Rom. 2:6; Matt. 16:27). **We must not allow ourselves to be consumed by hatred, a vendetta, or bitterness. Instead we hand over our pain to the Lord who will one day make things right. In the end, good will most certainly triumph over evil.

---

[99] Oden, p. 173; Walter Lock, *The Pastoral Epistles* (Edinburgh: T&T Clark, 1936.), p. 118.

[100] Mounce, p. 1196; Fee, p. 245; Knight, p. 467; I Clement 5.2,5.

5. Always remember, the *Lord will stand by you, and will rescue you*. (4:16-18)

What a life-freeing principle!

1) This truth enables us to forgive the seemingly unforgivable.

When Rome burned in A. D. 64, Nero blamed it on the Christians and began to persecute them. Subsequently, it became dangerous to be labeled a Christian in Rome. Filled with fear, local believers, and even Paul's coworkers, deserted him, refusing to be witnesses for the defense at his trial. Their abandonment was a deep disappointment for Paul. Hughes exclaims, "The situation was pathetic, scandalous! Here was the great missionary general, who had weathered the storms of several continents for the gospel, standing at the end alone before the Roman court."[101]

As striking as the abandonment is Paul's prayer that this will not be held against them in the final judgement. What astonishing forgiveness! One must immediately ask, "How can this be?" Two reasons are given:

When others would not, *the Lord stood by me*. In the absence of his friends, he experienced the overwhelming presence of the friend that never leaves us or forsakes us — *the greatest friend of all* — his Savior and Lord. In that moment, the promise was fulfilled, "when you walk through the fire (like the three Hebrews in the fiery furnace), when you pass through the waters (like Israel in the Red Sea), I will be with you. (Isaiah 43:2). We are NEVER alone!

When others could not, *the Lord strengthened me*. With the divine omnipresence comes the divine omnipotence. God unleashed His power within Paul enabling him to speak, at his hearing, with boldness,

---

[101] Hughes, p. 4869.

and to deliver a robust, comprehensive, personal testimony that would reach far beyond Nero's court room to Italy and the surrounding gentile world.

Perhaps all this caused Paul to reflect on God's sovereignty, who allowed him to go through this alone. Why? So, the world could see that it was God, and God alone that rescued him from *the lion's mouth*, meaning the emperor, Nero. Just as it was with Joseph, when others did him no good, it became an opportunity for God to accomplish the greatest good — reaching countless more with the good news of the gospel. This truth enabled him to forgive despite the circumstances.

2)   This truth gives us a forever hope when all seems hopeless.

The *Lord will rescue me*. I can count on it, rest in it. The forces of evil cannot destroy me. For even if they take my life, in that moment I will be brought safely into the very presence, the eternal kingdom of God. God ultimately "delivers us from every evil." When Satan throws everything in his arsenal at us, he fails. We have an inheritance that cannot be extinguished or stolen. It cannot be tainted or defiled. It will shine with the dazzling brilliance of the light of God's glory never to lose its luster, never to lose its incomparable joy.[102] No wonder we shout glory!

6. For believers to believers, there are no *final greetings*! (4:19-22).

Paul's exit will soon be an entrance. But as he goes, he reminds us of our friendships both now and in the future.

A)   *We would not be where we are without friends.* They are significant in every part of our lives. Prisca and Aquilla were seemingly wealthy business owners (tentmakers or leather workers), with

---

[102] I Peter 1:4-5

whom he found employment and lodging in Corinth (Acts 18:1-4). These loyal friends joined him when he left Corinth and stayed in Ephesus. While there, they became instrumental in discipling Apollos, refining, and enlarging this gifted teacher's understanding of the ways of God (18:24-26). Romans 16:4 tells us, they "even risked their necks" for Paul, when his life was in imminent danger. Later, they are instrumental in establishing a house church in Rome (Rom. 16:5).

As we saw in 1:16-17, the household of Onesiphorus had repeatedly entertained and provided refreshment for Paul. They were among the company of the unashamed who saw Paul's imprisonment as a badge, not a blemish, an opportunity, not an obstacle.

Little is known of Erastus and Trophimus. What we do know is that they were co-workers. The former remains doing ministry in Corinth (See Acts 19:22; Rom. 16:23). The latter is ill. At the very least, Paul is informing Timothy of colleagues of whom he had known or heard. Every friend, no matter how seemingly inconsequential, is to be respected as part of our salvation journey.

As Paul closes the letter, he sends greetings from members, possibly even leaders of the church at Rome. One is a woman, Claudia, and tradition says that Linus became the Bishop of Rome following Peter.[103]

B) *Our friendships will one day include countless saints, we have never previously met, in eternity.* The new heaven and new earth will give innumerable opportunities to develop and grow rich friendships. Imagine talking and fellowshipping with Mary, the mother of Jesus, Esther, Ruth, Paul, Peter, Timothy, John...The list goes on and on! Ancestors we have never met, people of every race, tribe, tongue, and nation, will one day partner with us in relationships deeper and more wonderful than we can ever imagine.

---

[103] Irenaeus, *Against Heresies* 3.3.3; Eusebius, *Ecclesiastical History* 3.2, 13.

To his *friend Timothy* comes the parting prayer, *the Lord be with your spirit.* To the larger body of the redeemed, *friends in the family, Grace to you (all)!*

But what does it mean for the Lord to be with your spirit? For Timothy, and for us, it is a petition for God to: 1) Manifest His presence within us as he goes with us; 2) Ignite passion, empowering, protecting, and assuring our ability to perform the particular ministry God has given us to do; and 3) Help us to maintain the purity of life and doctrine that effective ministry requires.

When we wish God's grace to someone we do so understanding that: 1) Grace comes not from ourselves, but from God; 2) We are asking for a future grace, starting right now, regardless of God's graces in the past; and 3) We desire the Holy Spirit to continue His work of grace in revealing God, illuminating His Word, convicting/convincing of sin, giving new life, gifting, indwelling, infilling, empowering, guiding, sanctifying, assuring, and unifying the church.

To our friends right now, and those about to pass on, we sing the lyrics of Michael W. Smith in his song, "Friends."

Packing up the dreams God planted

In the fertile soil of you

Can't believe the hopes He's granted

Means a chapter in your life is through

But we'll keep you close as always

It won't even seem you've gone

'Cause our hearts in big and small ways

Will keep the love that keeps us strong...[104]

---

[104] Go to https://www.youtube.com/watch?time_continue=26&v=H0Zaevi3IUw&-feature=emb_logo

Chapter Ten
Conclusion Unashamed and Unafraid

As I write, Christian thinking and Christian living are coming under fire. Widespread paranoia is being fueled by suspicions of a "civil war" between the radical left and the evangelical "right." Our biblical values are daily assaulted using blatant falsehoods, distortions, gross misunderstandings, intimidation, verbal, and physical persecution. Ubiquitous bashing and mocking have become a part of the "everyday menu" of television, the movies, and social media.

But, in the thick of all this, we stand tall, unashamed, and unafraid. We stand on the shoulders of those who have gone before us with faces like flint, with unwavering determination to persevere for the sake of the gospel. They were unafraid, unashamed in life and in death. These voices from the past echo courage and steely resolve, even as, for many, we hear the voice of their blood cry to God from the ground.

As a young pastor, I remember going to hear Lutheran minister, Richard Wurmbrand, recount the atrocities he experienced while imprisoned in a Romanian Gulag for fourteen years. Tears filled my eyes as he spoke of the guards urinating on crosses and down his mouth; forced marches, naked for miles through the snow; ferocious dogs, ready to tear him apart; and being held by chains within inches of his body. Then there was the starvation diet, including spoiled food with maggots crawling in it; being thrown into a very tight cell with walls lined with steel spikes; the torture of having to stare for hours at a high-gloss painted wall with a spotlight shining on it; and the years of beatings and solitary confinement.

But his reaction to all he had been through was not what I was ready to hear. When one would expect a seething hatred toward his "communist" torturers, what swelled up from his inner being was an unfathomable love for the souls of his captors. God had placed a fire of compassion in his heart that they could not snuff out.

To stand tall is also to love all. It is at the very center of our faith. This is the shame-freeing message we want the opponents of our gospel to hear. We do not stand, must not stand, with the fervor of supercilious elitists snooting our snobbery as we look down on them "from the heavens." This is not the way of Christ. He came not to be served, but to serve and to give His life for many (Mark 10:45). One of our greatest "weapons" is providing for those in need of the most basic life-sustaining necessities, for those who are marginalized, those in prison *physically and spiritually,* for the ostracized, and for the sick and afflicted (Matt. 25: 35-40). We come with the love saturated message that will free the captives of addictions, broken relationships, abusive situations, bigotry, and hatred.

We love because we were loved even though much about us was unlovable. God loved us even when we were His enemies living in willful rebellion (Rom. 5:8). The grace that saves us is amazing, undeserved, costly, yet freely given. How then can we possibly, pridefully, see one race as better than another, place one economic group over all others, or believe one nation to be more loved by God than others? God loves the whole world! Was it not the sin of pride that brought down Satan, his angels, and Adam and Eve in the garden?

It is also our love that compels us to give the *whole gospel,* not just one side of the gospel. God is not only a God of love, and mercy, He is also a God of holiness and justice. We cannot simply pick the aspect of God that we choose. In the unity of God's person, no one characteristic of God can be seen to be more important than another, but simply one aspect of His total harmonious nature.[105] He is both perfectly loving and holy at the same time and at all times.

God in His holiness, absolute purity of character, loves all that is right and good. Since sin brings destruction to everything it touches, it threatens all that God has created. Therefore, He must certainly deplore every threat to that love. And, in order to do what is just and right — what is true to his nature — sin must be punished.

That is a problem for each, and everyone, of us. We are all habitual sinners by nature (Rom. 3:10; 3:23). There is a rottenness in us that goes to the very core of our being. We not only commit acts of sin (Gal. 5:19-21), but we also have a pervasive attitude of sin, willful rebellion and hostility to God's commands and desires for us (Rom. 8:7-8). It is that very desire for total independence that brings so much physical, emotional, relational, and spiritual pain into our lives. It is also the root of our hostility toward the servants of God and His designs for sex, gender, marriage, and social interaction.

As we have seen, God has provided a remedy for our sin both now, and in eternity. Since entrance into heaven and enjoyment of the coming new earth, demands absolute purity of life, we are hopeless to meet God's standard. Therefore, God lovingly sent His Son, Jesus, to live the perfect life His holiness demanded, and to pay the full penalty for our sin by dying on the cross (John 3:16; Rom. 5:8). Our part is to admit that we are sinners in need of His love and grace, to receive His free gift of salvation in the person of Christ, and to turn from our old destructive way of life to a new abundant life in Christ (Rom. 10:9-10).

How can I possibly be ashamed of this gospel? How can I not love a God who at every turn has given and gives fully and wholly of Himself to others? How can I not proclaim the good news of a future where every negative, disastrous effect of sin will forever be removed from creation? How can I not thrill at the thought of perfect vibrant, totally

---

[105]Grudem, p. 206-209.

fulfilling relationships in the new heaven and new earth? How can I not look with expectancy to the coming King of Kings who will bring the worldwide peace for which we all look? Shout it loud; sound it far: I am not ashamed; I am unafraid, and you can be too!

Part Two

Shame-free Pathways
Devotionals

Kimberly Allston

Table of Contents

WEEK 1-
BACKGROUND FOR 2 TIMOTHY

INTRODUCTION The book of 2 Timothy is a letter written from a mentor to a mentee. At the writing of this Bible book, Paul (the mentor) has been engaged in ministry work with Timothy (his mentee) for approximately 16 years. Their friendship is a part of God's plan to strengthen each other's spiritual life as well as spread the gospel to the nations. They have had a full ministry together of sharing Jesus and developing other disciples. The relationship between these two Godly men has become like a father and son. Paul has taught Timothy all he knows about ministry, missions, and the gospel. The relationship has been foundational to both of their lives but is now about to end.

Since Paul is in prison and sentenced to die soon, it will be Timothy's responsibility to carry on their mission of spreading the gospel. Timothy's sorrow over Paul's separation and worry of fulfilling the ministry work is set to be one of the darker periods of his life. He is filled with doubt, frustration, discouragement, and burden. He will have to savor the Savior and move into action with all that Paul has taught him to carry on the ministry.

Can you ever remember a time when you were completely unafraid and unashamed? Just being one of those would be an accomplishment, but both - at the same time? I can count on one hand when I was completely unafraid and unashamed at the same time. In our unfriendly

85

world today, it can be quite a struggle to be unafraid and unashamed, but Paul lived a life free of fear and shame. What an example he is to us. So, what makes Paul different? How did he manage to live so boldly? How can we learn from him? What was his secret?

As we journey together through the book of 2 Timothy, we will discover one man sharing his heart and experiences with another man for the purpose of living free of fear and shame.

Second Timothy is a letter written from Paul to Timothy; from mentor to mentee; from pastor to pastor; from friend to friend.

Second Timothy is also a letter written to you and me. It is a letter that outlines how we can learn to live a life free of fear and shame in such a hostile world.

FROM INFORMATION TO TRANSFORMATION

To fully understand the depth of Paul and Timothy's relationship, we must go to the beginning. Paul's story is especially unique since he first killed Christians before becoming one himself. His background highlights quite the story of redemption. The man we first meet in Acts is quite different than the man we meet in 2 Timothy.

It is a story that completely changes everything about him including his name. It is a story that reveals how one man who becomes completely changed can completely change the world. A man who learns to be unafraid and unashamed can teach us how to be the same.

Paul's previous mission was clear — torture and kill as many Jesus followers as possible. In his mind, he was serving the God he knew and loved. Paul had grown up in a religious Jewish family, studied the Old Testament and followed the God of Abraham. He was disgusted with Christians who claimed that Jesus was the Messiah. He felt that these heretics were destroying the Jewish faith by claiming this man Jesus was performing miracles with God's power. Paul thought he was preserving the Jewish law and serving his God by physically destroying those who believed in this mere man who died on a tree. These followers had to be stopped. They had to be silenced.

Paul had no idea that this Jesus was about to intervene in stopping and silencing him. Paul (formerly known as Saul) is on his way to Damascus to prey on more Jesus followers.

Acts 9:3-9 (NIV)

> "As he neared Damascus on his journey, suddenly a light from heaven flashed around him. He fell to the ground and heard a voice say to him, 'Saul, Saul, why do you persecute me?' 'Who are you, Lord?' Saul asked. 'I am Jesus, whom you are persecuting,' he replied. 'Now get up and go into the city, and you will be told what you must do.' The men traveling with Saul stood there speechless; they heard the sound but did not see anyone. Saul got up from the ground, but when he opened his eyes, he could see nothing. So, they led him by the hand into Damascus. For three days he was blind and did not eat or drink anything."

You've just read the transformation of Paul. Jesus had to take drastic measures to get Paul's attention. Jesus had to literally knock Paul off his feet. Until this encounter with Jesus, Paul only had information. There was no connection, no relationship, no understanding of the Son of God. As with all of us, Paul had a special calling on his life. However, he was missing the right mission. Paul thought he was on the right mission, but Jesus had to show him in a very intense way that the mission he was on was not the right one.

What mission are we on? We may think we're on our best mission but really, it's just a busy mission — a mission that keeps us in the worldly rat race but not the righteous race for Christ.

Jesus used the information that Paul had and transformed it into a life: real life; bold life; giving life; eternal life.

Paul had no idea how long he would be blind. The scripture tells us that it was for three days, but Jesus never told Paul how long it would be. What do you think those three days were like for him? Paul had been spiritually blind and now he was physically blind.

The experience had been so intense that Paul did not eat or drink. He was blind and emotionally paralyzed. His beliefs had changed; his perspective had changed; his mission had changed; HE had changed. Jesus told Paul to go into the city and he would be told what to do. Notice that Jesus did not tell Paul immediately what he must do. Paul had to wait. Transformation often happens in the waiting, in the detours of life. This is how Jesus uses transformation. It's not something we can read about or study. It is something we must experience. It is an intense change in actions and beliefs.

Transformation is never easy.

Transformation is necessary for change.

Transformation becomes testimony.

Transformation is opportunity for growth.

Transformation is real.

Transformation is lasting.

Transformation leads to being unafraid and unashamed in an unfriendly world.

OBEY WITHOUT DELAY: THE ACTIONS OF ANANIAS

After Paul's encounter with Jesus, he is led to a house in Damascus. He has been blinded and is not eating and drinking. He is waiting on the Lord's instructions.

Meanwhile, the Lord is speaking to His servant, Ananias, and giving him instructions to go find Paul.

Acts 9:3-10-19 (NIV)

"In Damascus there was a disciple named Ananias. The Lord called to him in a vision, 'Ananias!' 'Yes, Lord,' he answered. The Lord told him, 'Go to the house of Judas on Straight Street and ask for a man from Tarsus named Saul, for he is praying. In a vision he has seen a man named Ananias come and place his hands on him to restore his sight.' 'Lord,' Ananias answered, 'I have heard many reports about this man and all the harm he has done to your saints in Jerusalem. And he has come here with authority from the chief priests to arrest all who call on your name.' But the Lord said to Ananias, 'Go! This man is My chosen instrument to carry My name before the Gentiles and their kings and before the people of Israel. I will show him how much he must suffer for My name.' Then Ananias went to the house and entered it. Placing his hands on Saul, he said, 'Brother Saul, the Lord — Jesus, who appeared to you on the road as you were coming here — has sent me so that you may see again and be filled with the Holy Spirit.' Immediately, something like scales fell from Saul's eyes, and he could see again. He got up and was baptized, and after taking some food, he regained his strength."

I love this heartfelt conversation between God and Ananias. Ananias genuinely wants to obey God but has a slight hesitation with the instructions. So many times, we want God's instructions to align with our thinking. But the truth is that God's instructions are always perfect and timely. We may think they don't make sense; they are messy; they are unimportant, or just not at the right time. God doesn't want just our thoughts in obedience to him; He also wants a willing heart. To obey him without our personal analysis.

In writing this book, I had more delay than obey. God had confirmed over and over that it was his will for me to write these devotions. It was I who had the problem. Even though Stan and I had written another book together, this one seemed so much harder. I had more fear than I had words to write. I kept making excuses. I even chose to clean the refrigerator drawers and shelves rather than write. Let me just tell you that I HATE cleaning the refrigerator. It's one of those dreaded tasks that I must make myself do.

Yet God kept gently reminding me that I was to write His words, not mine. I knew in my head that I had to rely on the Lord's strength but somehow that hadn't translated to my heart yet. I had to put faith before fear. I had to put faith over feelings.

How could I possibly be writing on the topic of being unafraid when I wasn't? Obedience is an action, not a feeling. If I was waiting on the time when I felt like writing, then I'd never get to it. I had to just sit down and open my heart and mind to what God wanted me to write.

Through Ananias, God showed me that delaying His instructions only increased the fear inside of me. God gave Ananias incredibly detailed instructions in dealing with Paul. Even though Ananias was clear on the instructions, He still wanted confirmation. God doesn't mind if we ask for confirmation; He just doesn't want us to ask for redirection.

Unbeknownst to Ananias, Paul had been transformed. God planned to use Ananias — "a man who was a devout observer of the law and highly respected by all the Jews living there," Acts 22:12 — to lay hands on Paul and prayerfully present him to the people as a vessel of God. Without Ananias' obedience, Paul's introduction to ministry would not have been ordained by God. With the credibility of Ananias, the Jews realized that Jesus had transformed Paul and he was now a follower of Christ, just like them.

Ananias didn't understand fully why God would send him to a known torturer of Christians. But God gave the same word to Ananias two times — GO! So much can be summed up in that one word. GO without analyzing My instructions; GO without questioning My plans; GO without putting your feelings first; GO without trusting in your own ability; GO without your flesh leading the way; GO without fear.

God is a GO-God. The word go is in His name.

To GO with God — is it our daily habit or daily hindrance?

Side Note: The Ananias we just read about is a different Ananias than the one mentioned in Acts chapter 5.

ALONE IN ARABIA

After Paul's conversion, he knew he had to grow in his relationship with Christ. The Lord had a reason for choosing Paul for this mission, and Paul had to become ready for his mission.

For Paul to become the man God wanted him to be, he had to spend time alone with Him. He had to get to know God in a very personal way that would lay a foundation to sustain many trials in the future. Paul had to know the character of God, trust in the character of God and share the character of God. There was no way to accomplish this except to be alone with God — just Paul and God — alone together in Arabia.

Paul writes in Galatians 1:11-18:

> "I want you to know, brothers, that the gospel I preached is not something that man made up. I did not receive it from any man, nor was I taught it; rather, I received it by revelation from Jesus Christ. For you have heard of my previous way of life in Judaism, how intensely I persecuted the church of God and

tried to destroy it. I was advancing in Judaism beyond many Jews of my own age and was extremely zealous for the traditions of my fathers. But when God, who set me apart from birth and called me by His grace, was pleased to reveal His Son in me so that I might preach Him among the gentiles, I did not consult any man, nor did I go up to Jerusalem to see those who were apostles before I was, but I went immediately into Arabia and later returned to Damascus. Then after three years, I went up to Jerusalem to get acquainted with Peter and stayed with him fifteen days."

If we want to be unafraid, we have to be alone with God.

If we want to be unashamed, we have to be alone with God.

We're all familiar with the story of the three little pigs. The first pig builds his house out of straw and it gets blown down; the second pig builds his house out of sticks and it gets blown down; the third and wisest pig builds his home out of solid brick and it keeps standing against the evil wolf.

The only way we can have a solid foundation with Christ is to have daily alone time with Him. This commitment continues to strengthen us when the heavy winds blow our way. Without this alone time, we can easily be drifting in no direction.

Paul knew the value of being alone with Jesus. He had to prepare himself for the future journey that God called him to.

There is no sugar coating it. If you want a strong foundation, a powerful transformation, a life that is unafraid and unashamed, you have to have alone time with the Lord. No excuses.

Do you know the story of Hezekiah in the Old Testament? It is one of my favorite Bible stories. Hezekiah was king of Judah over God's people. The Bible tells us that King Hezekiah received a letter from the opposing king of Assyria. In the letter, the king writes that he is coming to destroy Hezekiah and his people. He even taunts Hezekiah and mocks him for his strong belief in God.

There is no doubt that Hezekiah felt the burden of that letter and the threat of defeat. What did Hezekiah do? Did he seek counsel from his military advisors? Did he respond with a threatening letter of his own? Did he hide in the castle, pacing the floor and living in fear?

NO! He didn't do any of those things.

Second Kings 19:14 says, "Hezekiah received the letter from the messengers and read it. Then he went up to the temple of the Lord and spread it out before the Lord. And Hezekiah prayed to the Lord."

Hezekiah went immediately to be alone with God and pray. He knew where the true power was. He knew the value of being alone with God and receiving His wisdom above all others. He knew there would be no victory without knowing the will of God.

The answer was being alone with God and Hezekiah knew it. God honored Hezekiah's commitment to him and protected all the city from the Assyrians.

Just like Hezekiah and Paul, we must commit to our alone time with God. Whether in a temple, or in Arabia, or our living room, or our car, God wants our full attention. There are tons of books on developing your quiet time with God, but the best answer is the simplest one — prayer and reading the Bible. Being in prayer with God means both talking and listening. Reading the Bible means seeking His truth and living it out. Don't let the enemy fill you with lies that you're too busy, or God understands that you can't give Him time, or your prayers aren't important. Your time alone with God is crucial. He wants that time with you.

Don't get blown away; make time to pray!

THE ENCOURAGERS HALL OF FAME

I distinctly remember the first time I learned about Barnabas. My father preached a sermon on him and said that Barnabas was a natural encourager. He said the name Barnabas means Son of Encouragement. My dad said that Barnabas lived up to his name so well that he would be in the encourager's hall of fame. I've always loved that description of Barnabas.

Barnabas played a huge role in Paul's life. Without Barnabas's encouragement, Paul's beginning ministry would have been quite different.

We first meet Barnabas in Acts 4:36-37:

> "Joseph, a Levite from Cyprus, whom the apostles called Barnabas (which means Son of Encouragement), sold a field he owned and brought the money and put it at the apostles' feet."

These verses tell us that Barnabas not only encouraged people with his words but also with his actions. He knew that his possessions belonged to God. He gave those possessions to God to be used to help others and give God the glory. Barnabas is a man of truth and action. He is such a great example for us today.

We don't know the exact time that Paul first met Barnabas, but we do know that Barnabas believed in Paul's integrity to the mission for Christ. Acts 9:26-27 says "When Paul came to Jerusalem, he tried to join the disciples, but they were all afraid of him, not believing that he really was a disciple. But Barnabas took him and brought him to the apostles. He told them how Saul on his journey had seen the Lord and that the Lord had spoken to him, and how in Damascus he had preached fearlessly in the name of Jesus."

Barnabas believed in Paul before anyone else. He was willing to stop long enough to see the Holy Spirit inside of Paul. Barnabas was a fruit inspector and saw much fruit of the spirit in Paul. He knew Paul had been changed by Christ.

Barnabas wasn't one to follow the crowd. He made his own decisions based on his relationship with the Holy Spirit. He was a man of action and truth — God's truth above man's truth. The reality was that the disciples (Jesus' hand-picked followers) were afraid of Paul and didn't want to believe that he had truly changed.

But Paul had changed. With Barnabas's encouragement, Paul was able to develop friendships with the disciples and join with them in sharing the gospel of Jesus Christ.

How would things have been different if Barnabas hadn't taken the time to encourage Paul and speak to the disciples on his behalf? Barnabas, Mr. Encourager, knew the value of standing with God's chosen. Barnabas was able to see beyond Paul's past and look at the changed man he had become. Praise God that He sees beyond our past and loves us all the same.

God often sends us encouragement through other people, but we must be careful not to seek other's encouragement over God's encouragement. He is the creator of encouragement. His encouragement will sustain us far longer than any human encouragement.

I think Paul would have done the Lord's work with or without the encouragement of Barnabas and the disciples. Yet, the Lord knew the value and blessing of sending Paul someone who was in his corner, someone that had his back, someone that stuck up for him.

I love the story of Barnabas because he stood by his convictions and wasn't swayed by the opinions of others. It would have been a lot easier to go with the crowd and judge Paul for his past actions, but Barnabas wasn't one to go with the crowd. He followed the leading of the Holy Spirit and used His God-given gift of encouragement to build up another believer. It makes me wonder how our world, our neighborhoods, our churches, our workplaces, our schools would be different if we constantly made the effort to build each other up instead of tearing each other down.

Paul later wrote in his letter to the people of Thessalonica, "Therefore encourage one another and build each other up" (1 Thess. 5:11). Paul knew the importance of encouragement. He talks about it many times in the Bible. As we receive encouragement from the Lord, we should share it with others. Encouragement is not something we keep to ourselves. It is meant to be shared repeatedly.

We all need a Barnabas in our lives. We all need to be a Barnabas in someone's life.

WEEK 2 –
DAILY DEVOTIONS: 2 TIMOTHY

Chapter 1
MENTOR MEETS MENTEE

2 TIMOTHY 1:1-4

"Paul, an apostle of Christ Jesus by the will of God, according to the promise of life that is in Christ Jesus, to Timothy, my dear son: Grace, mercy and peace from God the Father and Christ Jesus our Lord. I thank God, whom I serve, as my forefathers did, with a clear conscience, as night and day I constantly remember you in my prayers. Recalling your tears, I long to see you, so that I may be filled with joy."

CHALLENGE:

Does God Think Mentorships Are Important?

INSPIRATION:

Acts 16:1-5:

"He (Paul) came to Derbe and then to Lystra, where a disciple named Timothy lived, whose mother was a Jewess and a believer, but whose father was a Greek. The brothers at Lystra and Iconium spoke well of him. Paul wanted to take him along on the journey, so he circumcised him because of the Jews who lived in that area, for they all knew that his father was a Greek. As they traveled from town to town, they delivered the decisions reached by the apostles and elders in Jerusalem for the people to obey. So, the churches were strengthened in the faith and grew daily in numbers."

Timothy had such a great reputation that Paul immediately included him on the missionary journey. Through God's perfect timing, both men would have their lives changed for the better. A relationship would develop between them that would last until Paul's death.

There were other Christian brothers on the missionary journey with Paul, so why did he choose Timothy to mentor? Honestly, I don't think mentorship was on Paul's mind at first. He wanted faith-filled men to travel with him to spread the gospel message. Through time, Paul could see that Timothy had a heart of faith and obedience. He could see that the Holy Spirit chose Timothy for pastoral work. Paul followed the leading of the Holy Spirit and poured his life into Timothy. Over the years, Timothy would become like a son to Paul.

Timothy was able to travel with Paul and learn how to minister. By the time Paul wrote the letter of 2 Timothy, the two had been mentor and mentee for approximately 16 years. Sadly, when Paul was writing this letter, he knew he was living in his last days.

From Warren Wiersbe's book, "Be Faithful," he writes, "When Paul wrote the letter we know as 2 Timothy, his situation had changed drastically. He was now a prisoner in Rome and was facing certain death. For one reason or another, almost all of Paul's associates in the ministry were gone and only Luke was at the apostle's side to assist him. It was a dark hour indeed. But Paul's great concern was not himself; it was Timothy and the success of the gospel ministry."

At that time, Timothy was ministering at Ephesus, but Paul requested Timothy to come see him one last time in Rome. Unfortunately, they would not have the chance to reunite before Paul's execution.

I'm sure Timothy would always treasure the last letter that Paul wrote to him. Paul writes in 2 Timothy 1: "Paul, an apostle of Christ Jesus by the will of God, according to the promise of life that is in Christ Jesus. To Timothy, my dear son: Grace, mercy and peace from God the Father and Christ Jesus our Lord. I thank God, whom I serve, as my forefathers did, with a clear conscience, as night and day I constantly remember you in my prayers. Recalling your tears, I long to see you, so that I may be filled with joy."

Wow — what an outpouring of love from Paul to Timothy. Paul acknowledges Timothy as a son, so their relationship had certainly evolved from mentor and mentee. I can only imagine the joy in Timothy's heart to read that not only is he like a son to Paul but also, he thanks God for him and constantly prays for him! There would be great joy from this letter but also great sorrow because Paul would be gone from Timothy's earthly life.

GOD'S TRUTH:

God wants us to have mentors and mentees in our life so we can learn more of His character and biblical truths.

I have had the great pleasure of having two wonderful mentors in my life, one being my co-author, Stan. He and his wife have been constant staples in my life for many years. We are all overjoyed when we get to be together. It's a friendship that doesn't require our guards to be up. We rejoice together, cry together, and carry each other's burdens. Stan is the most nonjudgmental man I have ever met. He is so humble and filled with the Holy Spirit. I have learned a great deal from this godly man. I have many notes in my Bible from his sermons. His understanding of the scriptures is amazing, and I always try to soak in as much as I can from him. Stan has helped me develop my gift of teaching scripture. He also has encouraged me by giving me opportunities to teach the Word. I knew that he believed in my ability to teach. He wanted me to get better in my gift of teaching.

My second great mentor was one of my Sunday School teachers, Sharon. She has the best balance of being both tough and tender. She would push me in my spiritual thinking and challenge me to know the scriptures. God aligned our paths in His perfect timing. I was praying for more opportunities to teach God's word and at the same time she was praying for someone to help her teach the Sunday School class. When she asked me to pray about helping her teach Sunday School, I immediately started crying because I knew that God had answered my prayer.

We have met many times to share and encourage each other. She has taught me so many truths. However, there is one meeting that stands out and will never be forgotten. Our time together started out like usual — catching up on our latest happenings, sharing what the Lord had been doing in our lives, and encouraging each other. Then the Lord took over and my mentor began speaking truth into an area of my life that needed attention. I had been struggling with a particular area for a while. I'd been praying about it but had convinced myself that my decision on the matter was justified. It was ok to do what I wanted until God had given me a clear answer, right? Certainly, God understood my dilemma and knew that I was only wanting to wait on Him, right? Can we say self-righteous complex?

My mentor gave me the tough truth talk that I needed to hear. She first pointed out what the Bible says about my situation. Isn't it amazing how the Bible addresses ALL situations for our lives? I had to realize that my situation wasn't unique, but my feelings were unique — there's a difference. She spoke very lovingly to me and really challenged me to look at my situation from God's perspective and not my own. She then asked me what truth I would give my daughter if she were the one in this situation and not me. Whoa — talk about a game changer. Just by changing my perspective, it allowed me to open my mind to how God was using my mentor to speak to me. After our meeting that day, I told the Lord that I had heard Him loud and clear as He spoke through my mentor.

YOUR TRUTH:

Do you have a desire to have a God-appointed mentor in your life?

Are you in a secure spiritual season to have a God-appointed mentee in your life?

As a mentee, what truths do you want to learn from a God-appointed mentor?

As a mentor, what truths do you have to share with a God-appointed mentee?

_____

_____

_____

_____

ACTION PLAN:

1. If you don't have a mentor, pray for the Lord to send the right person for you and your season of life right now. God has the perfect match for you — trust His timing.

2. If you are in a secure spiritual season, please pray for the Lord to send you the right mentee to build up in Christ. Wisdom is a gift from God for us to pass on — not keep for ourselves!

Qualities of a great mentor:

> A great mentor teaches you to rise up in your spiritual gifts, just as Paul wanted Timothy to get better in ministry. A mentor always wants the best for his/her mentee.

> A great mentor is both tough and tender. He/she wants to push you beyond your limits and soar in God's calling for your life.

> A great mentor will not want you to stay in your comfort zone. He/she wants to make you aware of how much the enemy wants to destroy you while at the same time fill you with confidence that our almighty Savior will fight our battles.

> *God will lead you to the right person at just the right time — exactly as he did for Paul and Timothy.*

A WOMAN'S INFLUENCE

2 TIMOTHY 1:5

"I have been reminded of your sincere faith which first lived in your grandmother Lois and in your mother Eunice and, I am persuaded, now lives in you also."

CHALLENGE:

How can we allow God to use us as women of influence and sincere faith?

INSPIRATION:

It is no accident that Paul mentions Timothy's mother and grandmother in his letter. These two women had a huge influence on both Paul and Timothy. We are first introduced to Timothy's mother, Eunice, in Acts 16:1. "He (Paul) came to Derbe and then to Lystra, where a disciple named Timothy lived, whose mother was a Jewess and a believer, but whose father was a Greek."

Warren Wiersbe writes, "Lois, Timothy's grandmother, was the first one in the family won to Christ; then his mother, Eunice, was converted. Timothy's father was a Greek, so Eunice had not practiced the orthodox Jewish faith. However, Timothy's mother and grandmother had seen to it that he was taught the scriptures." Second Timothy 3:15 says, "and how from infancy you have known the holy scriptures, which are able to make you wise for salvation through faith in Christ Jesus."

I love that verse! First, it shows us how a mother and grandmother shared God's word with Timothy since he was a baby. What a beautiful commitment to read about. Second, God clearly tells us that His word will make us wise and faithful to Jesus.

If you are a mom or grandmother, don't ever stop teaching scripture to your precious loved ones. Scripture will impact lives!!!!

GOD'S TRUTH:

Lois and Eunice had no idea what plans God had for Timothy. Their faithful instruction and love of scripture would one day lead Timothy to minister with the most well-known missionary of all time. Their influence was instilled in Timothy one day at a time. Their love of the scripture transferred to Timothy and prepared him for his God given assignment later in life.

Make no mistake — a woman's influence is powerful!!! It can be used for either good or for evil. In Mark 6, we are told that a mother named Herodias had great hatred for John the Baptist. One day Herodias' daughter won favor from King Herod and was granted anything that she wanted. When the daughter asked her mother, Herodias, what she should ask for, her mother said to ask the king for the head of John the Baptist on a platter. The king granted the wish and gave the daughter

John's head on a platter which she immediately gave to her mother. A woman's influence used for evil.

We have just read examples of both extremes — influence used for good and influence used for evil. Even if the story of Herodias seems extreme to you, please understand that whatever sin is in our hearts can build up and lead to a domino of sin. We must be extremely careful in guarding our hearts against the enemy who will do anything to destroy us and our families. John 10:10 says, "The thief comes only to steal and kill and destroy; I (Jesus) have come that they may have life and have it to the full." One way that the enemy likes to hinder us is through complacency. We have put the spiritual development of our children on the back burner. We lie to ourselves in thinking that taking kids to church is enough. That is one of the biggest lies that Satan has used against us. One hour a week in church will not give your children the influence they need to live to the full in Jesus.

YOUR TRUTH:

How are you a woman of influence? How does your influence align with God's truths and purposes?

_____

_____

_____

_____

ACTION PLAN:

Women immerse yourself and your children/grandchildren in the scriptures. Living a life in Jesus and knowing His character will influence and impact a person's life like nothing else. Please get off the busy merry-go-round and make scriptures a priority.

As a mom to three, I know how hard it is to become rooted in the scriptures every day. After years of trying different family devotions and having guilt for not being consistent with them, I finally gave this burden over to the Lord. I asked Him what and when would work best for our family. He so gently revealed to me that family devotion time is not a box on the to-do list that you check off. It's a lifestyle!!! Progress not perfection. It is bringing Jesus into our everyday conversations, reading how prayer changed the lives of so many people in the Bible, discussing the difference between living for the world and living in the Word.

It was a long road, but finally I have peace in the process of influencing my children for life with Jesus. God knows our hearts and our motives. He has all the answers. Let Him show you how to be a powerful woman of influence — one step at a time: one day at a time.

FOCUS ON HIS POWER

2 TIMOTHY 1:7-8

Today we will be looking closely at one of the most popular verses in the Bible. Let us review the different translations of these important verses.

<u>NIV</u>:

> "For this reason, I remind you to fan into flame the gift of God, which is in you through the laying on of my hands. *For God did not give us a spirit of timidity, but a spirit of power, of love and of self-discipline.*"

<u>New King James</u>:

> "Therefore, I remind you to stir up the gift of God which is in you through the laying on of my hands. *For God has not given us a spirit of fear, but of power and of love and of a sound mind.*"

New American Standard:

> "For this reason, I remind you to kindle afresh the gift of God
> which is in you through the laying on of my hands. *For God
> has not given us a spirit of timidity, but of power and love and
> discipline.*"

The Message:

> "And the special gift of ministry you received when I laid hands
> on you and prayed-keep that ablaze! *God doesn't want us to be
> shy with His gifts, but bold and loving and sensible.*"

CHALLENGE:

How do we use our God-given gifts without being stricken with a
spirit of fear?

INSPIRATION:

The book of 2 Timothy is like a giant puzzle. Each verse is a puzzle
piece that fits another piece to reveal the full puzzle of God's master
plan for His children in living out an unashamed and unafraid life in
an unfriendly world. God wants to build and grow our spiritual character. These verses are our battle plan to use God's strength in the gifts
He has given us.

So, let's break down this verse and dig deep into its meanings. John
MacArthur, Jr. writes in his 2 Timothy commentary "that any spirit of
timidity we might have is not from God. It is cowardly, shameful fear
that is generated by weak, selfish character. The Lord is never responsible
for our cowardice, our lack of confidence, or our being shameful of Him."

We must make the effort to obey God even when we are afraid.
Unfortunately, we can easily allow our fears to be motivated by

selfishness. God knows our weaknesses. In fact, 'fear not' is found over 300 times in the Bible. God has to consistently remind us not to focus on our fear but to focus on Him.

GOD'S TRUTH:

Trusting God does not mean we will never be afraid. True faith is when we can take that next step, leave our comfort zone and walk in obedience even though we don't know where the road will lead.

Paul knew that Timothy was afraid, so he encouraged him to focus on God and not his flesh. But why did Paul choose the next three words of power, love and self-discipline? Why are these three words so important to use when tapping into God's strength? We first must understand that God is the giver of these, and we are the receivers. It is God Himself who did not give us the spirit of timidity but instead gave us the spirit of power, love and self-discipline.

John MacArthur, Jr. continues to share that "the resources we have from our heavenly Father are power and love and discipline. When we are apprehensive, we can be sure it is because our focus is on ourselves and our own human resources rather than on the Lord and His available divine resources." This all sounds great on paper but how do we apply it to our daily lives?

1. First, we must check and re-check our motives when using our gifts. Even if you are not clear yet on your God-given gifts, what will be your motivation for using them when they are discovered? With these gifts that God has given us, are we using them for our own glory or for His? Do we take the credit or acknowledge Him? Is our heart humble or proud?

2. Second, embrace the freedom and gift that nothing (and I mean nothing) relies on us except our obedience to God. He is the one who will bring the power, love, and discipline when we need it

the most. Give up the control because He can handle ALL our circumstances a lot better than we can.

3.   Third, commit to abiding in the Lord EVERY DAY!!! Power, love and discipline are not attributes that we only need once a week. These are DAILY principles for our lives. This means that we must lean into the Lord every day to receive them. God gives us just enough for each day (our daily bread). He does this so we can stay humble and not start using our own strength. Daily abiding involves prayer and time in His Word. If these two things are not part of your everyday routine, then it is time to change your routine. Do not buy into our world's thinking that independence and self-reliance are the keys to success and happiness. This is a lie from the enemy. Given the choice, why would we ever choose our strength over God's strength? Our dependence on Him will give us so much more than we can ever gain by ourselves.

YOUR TRUTH:

Are you operating with a spirit of fear or spirit of power? How can you use God's strength to use your gifts with a spirit of love, power, and self-control?

_____

_____

_____

_____

ACTION PLAN:

MacArthur, Jr. goes on to say, "The great spiritual triumvirate of power, love and discipline belong to every believer. These are not natural endowments. We are not born with them, and they cannot be learned in a classroom or developed from experience. They are not the result of heritage or environment or instruction. But all believers possess these marvelous, God-given endowments; power, to be effective in His service; love, to have the right attitude toward Him and others; and discipline, to focus and apply every part of our lives according to His will." I love how this is broken down:

Power = effectiveness

Love = right attitude

Self-Discipline = focus

God used Paul to emphasize to Timothy and to us that He freely gives us everything we need to succeed in using our gifts for His glory. We are not cowards with selfish motives, we are believers in the Most High God ready to receive His power for our effectiveness, His love for our right attitude and His self-discipline for His focus. Onward!

GUARD THE GOSPEL

2 TIMOTHY 1:8-14

"So do not be ashamed to testify about our Lord, or ashamed of me his prisoner. But join with me in suffering for the gospel, by the power of God, who has saved us and called us to a holy life — not because of anything we have done but because of his own purpose and grace. This grace was given us in Christ Jesus before the beginning of time, but it has now been revealed through the appearing of our Savior, Christ Jesus, who has destroyed death and has brought life and immortality to light through the gospel. And of this gospel I was appointed a herald and an apostle and a teacher. That is why I am suffering as I am. Yet I am not ashamed, because I know whom I have believed, and am convinced that he is able to guard what I have entrusted to him for that day. What you heard from me, keep as the pattern of sound teaching with faith and love in Christ Jesus. Guard the good deposit that was entrusted to you — guard it with the help of the Holy Spirit who lives in us."

CHALLENGE:

How do we guard the gospel given to us from Christ Jesus?

INSPIRATION:

God not only offers His strength to help us guard the gospel, but He also encourages all of us to strengthen each other. Earlier in Paul and Timothy's ministry, Paul wrote a letter to the church in Corinth to answer their questions about the gospel and encourage them to remain faithful. In his letter he says, "If Timothy comes, see to it that he has nothing to fear while he is with you, for he is carrying on the work of the Lord, just as I am. No one, then, should refuse to accept him. Send him on his way in peace so that he may return to me. I am expecting him along with the brothers" (1 Cor. 16:10-11).

What a beautiful example of Paul's taking care of Timothy. It is a great example to us on how we can take care of each other as we do the work of the Lord. As Christ followers, are we accepting others in the work they are doing? Are we allowing a judgment-free atmosphere for others to carry on their work for the Lord? Are we blessing others with peace as they move forward with the Lord? Paul continues his encouragement in 1 Corinthians 10:13-14, "Be on your guard; stand firm in the faith; be men of courage; be strong. Do everything in love."

GOD'S TRUTH:

There are several key elements in these verses that help us become guards of the gospel.

1. A Call for Courageous Guards — God gives the call to us as well as the courage to live it out. God calls us all to live a holy life — a life focused on Him and sharing His love with others. Even though we all will suffer, God wants us to be courageous like Paul and endure the suffering with the courage that God freely gives.

2. Testifying the Truth — I love how Paul gets right to the point with Timothy. He doesn't try to sugar coat anything. He instructs Timothy not to be ashamed to testify about the Lord or be ashamed of Paul (who is in prison). In America, we do not have religious persecution on the same level as other countries. We don't live in fear of constant persecution for our religious beliefs. We are free to worship in freedom. This is a gift that most of the world does not have. Other Christians are being slaughtered every day for their faith in Jesus. Yet, these Christians are more open with their beliefs than most of us in America.

3. Confidence in Suffering — Why do we hate suffering and try to avoid it at all cost? God does not expect us to hide from the struggle. Paul not only tells Timothy to expect struggle, but he also tells him to join with him. Paul is so confident about the struggling because it is through the power of God that he will be comforted. Paul goes on to explain that he is not ashamed to suffer because he is secure in Christ's plan for his earthly life and heavenly life. We also hate to see our loved ones suffer and do everything in our power to protect them from struggling. However, protection from struggle also means we are robbing them of knowing God's strength.

4. Guarding the Truth — Paul doesn't mean guard the gospel and keep it to ourselves. He means to guard the purity of the gospel and do not let false teachers distort the fundamental truths. These fundamental truths are God's words outlined in the Bible that Jesus is His son and the only way to eternal life is through Jesus (John 3:16).

YOUR TRUTH:

Using God's truth in this devotion, how do you guard the gospel in your daily life?

_____

_____

_____

_____

ACTION PLAN:

1. We need the help of the Holy Spirit to discern between truth and false teachings in order to guard the true gospel. There can be a fine line between true gospel and false gospel. Even Satan and his demons know what the scriptures say. If they know the scriptures better than you, then they can easily deceive you by changing God's word to fit their narrative. We can easily be led astray if we only rely on ourselves and not the full truth of God's word.

2. Read and study God's word daily to learn God's character.

3. Spend time in silence with God in order to discern His voice. This takes practice and patience but the more you listen to His voice, the more you are clear on what He is saying to you and are assured of truthful teaching.

REJECTION AND REASSURANCE

2 TIMOTHY 1:1:15-18

"You know that everyone in the province of Asia has deserted me, including Phygelus and Hermogenes. May the Lord show mercy to the household of Onesiphorus because he often refreshed me and was not ashamed of my chains. On the contrary, when he was in Rome, he searched hard for me until he found me. May the Lord grant that he will find mercy from the Lord on that day! You know very well in how many ways he helped me in Ephesus."

CHALLENGE:

Why does God allow us to experience the pain of rejection?

INSPIRATION:

As Paul writes in verse 15, he was extremely hurt by the rejection of so many, including Phygelus and Hermogenes. We don't know much about these two men, but Paul's pain is evident as he talks about their desertion of him. How disheartening it must have been for Paul to pour his heart into people only to be cast away when things got tough and he went to prison.

As much as Paul was hurt by rejection, he was also reassured and comforted by a friend that proved faithful. Paul's friend, Onesiphorus, did not turn his back when Paul was put in prison. On the contrary, Onesiphorus, searched for Paul until he found him. God knew that Paul needed reassurance and encouragement and used his servant, Onesiphorus, to refresh Paul during a dark time. This wasn't the first time that he had helped Paul. Onesiphorus also helped in Ephesus when Paul was preaching the gospel. This was a true friend who stuck by Paul through good times and bad. Paul is expressing to Timothy how grateful he is to have someone besides Jesus who is faithful to him.

In these verses, Paul explains that the Lord is so merciful. Even though we sometimes must endure rejection, the Lord also sends reassurance. In the book, *The Letters to Timothy, Titus and Philemon* by

William Barclay, it says, "Hermogenes and Phygelus go down to history branded as deserters; Onesiphorus goes down to his history as the friend who stuck closer than a brother. If we were to be described in one sentence, what would that one sentence be? Would a one-sentence verdict on our lives be the verdict on a traitor, or the verdict on a disciple who was true?"

GOD'S TRUTH:

Rejection is the pits. I have always struggled with rejection and the enemy knows it all too well. He never hesitates to use his power to trigger my feelings of rejection. Paul knew the pain of rejection and informed Timothy to expect it. We have all experienced rejection and will continue to experience it.

So why does God allow us to experience the pain of rejection? First, He gave us the comfort of knowing that our Savior, Jesus, knows exactly how rejection feels. All through His ministry and especially in His last days, He experienced great rejection — from his enemies as well as his closest friends. Because of this, He can empathize with our pain. We only must reach out to Him for His comfort. Second, God allows rejection in our lives so He can build our spiritual character. He wants us to rely on Him and never get too comfortable with this worldly culture. We always must remember that earth is not our home. Our eternal home is in heaven where there will be no rejection or hurt.

Rejection has been a staple in my life that I've always struggled with. I can still remember vividly being rejected by the 'popular' girls all through school. Those memories never leave us, but God's love can heal it. When we acknowledge the pain of rejection to our Savior, He uses the Holy Spirit to remind us that our identity is in Him. Painful memories may scar us, but they don't define us. Our identity is in Christ alone.

YOUR TRUTH:

How can you let God use your pain of rejection to heal yourself and others?

_____

_____

_____

_____

ACTION PLAN:

1. Embrace your pain of rejection.

2. Realize that the burden of rejection is not for you to carry; give it to the Lord.

3. Allow God to use the pain of rejection for His glory so we can relate to others and use opportunities to reassure others.

4. Jesus suffered the worst rejection so that we can have victory in our lives.

5. Meditate on Psalm 94:14: "For the Lord will not reject His people; He will never forsake His inheritance."

WEEK 3 –
DAILY DEVOTIONS: 2 TIMOTHY

Chapter 2
NO SHORTCUTS IN SACRIFICE

2 TIMOTHY 2:1-7

"You then, my son, be strong in the grace that is in Christ Jesus. And the things you have heard me say in the presence of many witnesses entrust to reliable men who will also be qualified to teach others. Endure hardship with us like a good soldier of Christ Jesus. No one serving as a soldier gets involved in civilian affairs — he wants to please his commanding officer. Similarly, if anyone competes as an athlete, he does not receive the victor's crown unless he competes according to the rules. The hardworking farmer should be the first to receive a share of the crops. Reflect on what I am saying, for the Lord will give you insight into all this."

CHALLENGE:

There are no shortcuts in life. In our last devotion, we experienced Paul's hurtful rejection and encouraging reassurance. Paul is now iterating to Timothy that life as a Christian will not be easy, and we must endure hardship in order to grow in our spiritual maturity. This is a huge challenge for Christ followers — how can we be strong in Christ while enduring hard times?

INSPIRATION:

Paul gives us the examples of a soldier, an athlete, and a farmer. None of them are immune to hard work and sacrifice and neither are we. The soldier must have singlemindedness in following orders from his commander and not become distracted with his own desires. An athlete must follow the rules if he wants to receive the reward. A farmer's hard work and dedication results in his receiving the first fruits of his labor. The inspiration for us is that we are not alone in living this life. Paul says to be strong in the grace of Christ which means that He is available to fill us with His strength that will long sustain past any of our strength. How exciting to know that Jesus freely gives His strength to us to endure our hardships. We don't have to do it by ourselves. Paul also inspires us by saying through reflection the Lord will also give us wisdom on these matters. A total win-win: the Lord's strength and wisdom!

GOD'S TRUTH:

You are NOT alone. Our lives will always include hardships, but the Lord never expects us to battle them alone. When we welcome His strength and wisdom, our journey becomes a companionship. The Lord expects our faithfulness and obedience to Him. Like the soldier, athlete, and farmer, there will be no shortcuts in the sacrifices but the rewards and blessings of spiritual maturity through the hard season will only enhance our relationship with our Jesus Christ.

YOUR TRUTH:

Write how your truth compares to God's truth relating to the top verses:

ACTION PLAN:

"You then, _____ (insert your name), be strong in the grace that is in Christ Jesus."

1. Discuss your hardship with Jesus.

2. Ask the Lord to fill you with His strength and wisdom to endure this time.

3. Memorize and consistently repeat the above verse with your name inserted.

Praise Him for how your life will receive the great rewards of enduring hardship while relying on Him.

CHRIST OVER COMFORT

2 TIMOTHY 2:8-13

"Remember Jesus Christ, raised from the dead, descended from David. This is my gospel, for which I am suffering even to the point of being chained like a criminal. But God's word is not chained. Therefore, I endure everything for the sake of the elect, that they too may obtain the salvation that is in Christ Jesus, with eternal glory."

Here is a trustworthy saying:

If we died with Him, we will also live with Him.

If we endure, we will also reign with Him.

If we disown Him, He will also disown us.

If we are faithless, He will remain faithful, for He cannot disown Himself."

CHALLENGE:

How do we consistently choose Christ over our own comforts?

INSPIRATION: Leah Sharibu

If you have not heard of Leah Sharibu, it is my incredible honor to share her story with you. At the age of 14, she was kidnapped from her school in Nigeria along with 109 of her classmates. The terrorist group, Boko Haram, released all the girls except for Leah because she was the only one who would not renounce Christ and convert to Islam.

Christ Over Comfort

In the book, *"Leah Sharibu: The Girl Boko Haram Left Behind,"* author Reno Omokri writes, "A group of radical Islamic terrorists, Boko Haram, is on a savage mission to end all forms of organized Western education in Nigeria. In keeping with their philosophy that Western education is sinful and the cause of most of society's ills, this group of misguided radicals have either burnt or otherwise destroyed 1500 schools and twice that number of churches. With their hatred for Western education, coupled with their disdain for Christianity, led this group to the town of Dapchi where they abducted 110 girls from Government Girls Science and Technical College, Dapchi, on Monday, February 19, 2018. Leah Sharibu was one of 110 girls that were taken."

Omokri continues, "On March 21, 2018, Boko Haram released 104 girls (five of the girls died either during abduction or while in captivity). Leah was not released." Leah was not released because she refused to convert to Islam.

Christ Over Comfort

On May 14, 2019, Leah celebrated her 16th birthday in captivity. No celebrations with her friends and family. No gifts. No special memories for a momentous milestone. BUT as a Christ follower with amazing courage, Leah knows all the rewards she will receive in eternity. She knows her eternal future is secure in Christ and no captivity will ever change that.

Christ Over Comfort

As of this writing, Leah is still believed to be alive and a prisoner of the terrorist group, Boko Haram. She is an extraordinary example to us of what it means to choose Christ over Comfort. We certainly do not understand why God is allowing her to suffer but we do know that He promises to bring good from all circumstances. "And we know that in all things God works for the good of those who love Him, who have been called according to His purpose" (Rom. 8:28).

Maybe the good will be at least one terrorist who sees the power of Christ in Leah and commits his life to the Savior. Maybe the good is all of Leah's family and community will become more committed to Christ and bring hope filled change to a corrupt government. Maybe the good will be an international movement of prayer warriors to flood God's throne for justice on the earth.

Christ Over Comfort

GOD'S TRUTH:

God is ALWAYS faithful.

We do not know the good God will use but we know He will use it. We can be comforted that He sees Leah; He has a plan for her and her family; He will bring freedom whether on this earth or in Heaven.

Paul also chose Christ over comfort since he was imprisoned for many years of his life. As he writes in the verses above, he suffered everything for others to know the saving power of Jesus Christ. God tells us that we all will suffer for Christ. As Christ followers, we are never immune from struggle. However, God freely gives His wisdom and strength to endure and remain faithful.

Hebrews 4:14-16 says, "Therefore, since we have a great high priest who has gone through the heavens, Jesus the Son of God, let us hold firmly to the faith we profess. For we do not have a high priest who is unable to sympathize with our weaknesses, but we have one who has been tempted in every way, just as we are — yet was without sin. Let us then approach the throne of grace with confidence, so that we may receive mercy and find grace to help us in our time of need." Amen!!

In order to choose Christ over comfort, we must fully surrender to His will and authority. Our lives are not our own. Our lives are His for His will, His timing, and His glory. We can take the examples of Paul and Leah to encourage us to trust God in all circumstances and draw on His strength during our struggle. The more we know God's word, the more we are freely able to surrender to His will. The more we know God's faithfulness, the more we can trust His timing. The more we know God's character, the more we can use our lives to glorify Him.

YOUR TRUTH:

In what area(s) of your life do you need to choose Christ over Comfort?

_____

_____

_____

_____

ACTION PLAN:

After first hearing about Leah's story, I went on the internet and printed out a picture of her to keep in my Bible. I wrote verses on the back of her picture to pray over her.

Please join me in praying these verses for Leah:

1. Hebrews 12:3 — "Consider Him who endured such opposition from sinful men, so that you will not grow weary and lose heart."

2. 2 Timothy 4:17 — "But the Lord stood at my side and gave me strength, so that through me the message might be fully proclaimed and all the [world] might hear it. And I was delivered from the lion's mouth."

3. Read more of Leah's story in "Leah Sharibu: The Girl Boko Haram Left Behind" by Reno Omokri.

4. Learn about the foundation created by Leah's parents:

    Leadership

    Empowerment

    Advocacy

    Humanitarian

5. Visit the website to learn how you can have a voice for Leah, contribute to the foundation and/or send encouraging letters to her parents — www.leah-foundation.org.

Choosing Christ over comfort is a daily choice.

It is a mindset, an attitude, a willful surrender despite our emotions and circumstances.

AVOID GODLESS CHATTER

2 TIMOTHY 2:14, 16-19, 23-24

"Keep reminding them of these things. Warn them before God against *quarreling about words*; it is of no value, and only ruins those who listen.

Avoid godless chatter because those who indulge in it will become more and more ungodly. Their teaching will spread like gangrene. Among them are Hymenaeus and Philetus, who have wandered away from the truth. They say that the resurrection has already taken place, and they destroy the faith of some. Nevertheless, God's solid foundation stands firm, sealed with this inscription: 'The Lord knows those who are His,' and, 'Everyone who confesses the name of the Lord must turn away from wickedness.'

Don't have anything to do with foolish and stupid arguments, because you know they produce quarrels. And the Lord's servant *must not quarrel*; instead, he must be kind to everyone, able to teach, not resentful."

CHALLENGE:

How can we avoid godless chatter?

INSPIRATION:

Many days in the Allston household, I think my kids could qualify for a master's degree in quarrels and arguments. Any little word, gesture, noise, or look can escalate the arguing and quarreling to epic proportions. So many times, the kids will purposefully say things to each other to aggravate and annoy. Why is it so hard to keep our mouths shut and not instigate a reaction? I constantly repeat Philippians 2:14 — "Do everything without complaining or arguing." Another important saying in our house is 'speak life or speak nothing'.

Paul considers quarreling and godless chatter as a serious problem since he mentions it to Timothy four times. The culture has not changed since Paul's day because we consistently deal with this problem. In a world dominated with social media, people have become amazingly comfortable spewing their hateful arguments towards others. Respectful dialogue and disagreement have almost become extinct. Paul is noticeably clear that followers of Jesus are called to a very high standard of communication and we must not,

1. Quarrel about words.

2. Engage in godless chatter.

3. Have anything to do with foolish and stupid arguments.

4. Quarrel.

GOD'S TRUTH:

Not only does God tell us to use our words carefully; He also tells us the why for those instructions.

1. It is of no value.

2. It ruins those who listen and can even destroy the faith of some.

3. It causes us to become more and more ungodly.

4. It will produce quarrels.

5. It prevents us from teaching others the salvation of Christ.

These are serious repercussions for those that indulge in godless chatter and quarreling. God is very clear on His instructions for being truth tellers. He freely gives us His strength to have a lifestyle of talking truth in love. God does not want us to never express ourselves or stay silent on important issues. Instead, He wants us to stand firm on His word and oppose others with Godliness. In an upcoming devotion, we will discuss God's instructions for confrontation and speaking truth in love.

YOUR TRUTH:

Write how your truth compares to God's truth relating to the top verses:

_____

_____

_____

_____

ACTION PLAN:

"_____ (insert your name), do everything without complaining or arguing."

1. Recognize the godless chatter and quarreling in your life.

2. Ask the Holy Spirit to alert you to respond in love when tempted to argue or speak godless chatter.

3. Continue in consistency because changing bad habits doesn't happen overnight.

THE FIGHT FOR FORTITUDE

FORTITUDE — courage in pain or adversity

2 TIMOTHY 2:15 — "Do your best to present yourself to God as one approved, a workman who does not need to be ashamed and who correctly handles the word of truth."

2 TIMOTHY 2:20-22 — "In a large house there are articles not only of gold and silver, but also of wood and clay; some are for noble purposes and some for ignoble. If a man cleanses himself from the latter, he will be an instrument for noble purposes, made holy, useful to the Master and prepared to do any good work. Flee the evil desires of youth and pursue righteousness, faith, love and peace, along with those who call on the Lord out of a pure heart."

CHALLENGE:

How can we remain clean and unashamed in God's eyes while living in a sin-filled world?

INSPIRATION:

If there was ever a time in the Bible that two people could say, "I told you so," it would be Joshua and Caleb. Soon after the exile from Egypt, the Lord gave instructions to His people to conquer and take possession of the land Canaan. Moses (the leader of the Israelites) sent spies into the land of Canaan to size up the enemy. Two of those spies were Joshua and Caleb. When all twelve spies returned from their forty-day mission, they reported to Moses. Ten of the spies told Moses, "We can't attack those people; they are stronger than we are. And they spread among the Israelites a bad report about the land they had explored" (Num. 13:32a). Not only did the ten spies allow fear to hinder their judgment, they also purposely spread fear among all the people. Only Joshua and Caleb told Moses and the people that "We should go up and take possession of the land, for we can certainly do it" (Num. 13:30b).

Because of fear and contempt, ten men caused severe consequences for the Israelites. The Lord struck down the ten men and they died of a plague. The Lord also said that "For forty years — one year for each of the forty days you explored the land — you will suffer for your sins and know what it is like to have Me against you" (Num. 14:34). Joshua and Caleb were the only two spies to survive and the only original Israelites to finally see the promised land of Canaan. However, they had to endure forty unnecessary years of wandering with grumbling, whiny, and faithless travelers.

Joshua and Caleb had every reason to remind the Israelites — "I told you so. You should have listened to us and invaded the land. We could have been living in the land of milk and honey if only you had more faith and less fear." How discouraging it must have been for Joshua and Caleb to hold strong to their faith while being trapped with the wavering and discontented people.

I am amazed at the fortitude of Joshua and Caleb. They stayed true to God during negativity. Their lives reflect what Paul wrote in verse 22— "flee evil desires and pursue righteousness with other strong believers." God blessed these two men by giving them each other during those forty years of turmoil. It is the same for us today. Our world is full of evil and negativity, yet God wants faithful hearts, not consistent excuses. We may have to swim with the sharks, but God always brings His faithful safely to shore. The fight for fortitude may be long but it is never in vain.

GOD'S TRUTH:

It's quite simple: God fights for those who are faithful to Him. As the verses in 2 Timothy above clarify, God wants followers who will never be ashamed of who He is and His plan of action for our lives. In these verses, Paul talks about items that are both valuable and invaluable. He is referring to people whose hearts are true to God versus those whose hearts are only true to themselves. Which one are you?

So many times, we only want to be faithful to God and His plans when they are convenient and approved by us. Are we an instrument willing to be used for noble purposes? Are we useful to our Master? Are we prepared to do any of His good work? We often want to know what God's plans are before we commit. We want to put conditions on the type of service we do in His name. We crave convenience and always want to compromise. It's only when we resolve ourselves to live a life of fortitude for the Lord's kingdom that we can truly enter the promise land of milk and honey.

When we are faithful and true to the right Master, then He can always use us for His glory, no matter where we are in life.

YOUR TRUTH:

Is your relationship with the one true God worth fighting for?

_____

_____

_____

_____

ACTION PLAN:

In Numbers 14:24, the Lord said this about Caleb: "But because my servant Caleb has a different spirit and follows me wholeheartedly, I will bring him into the land he went to, and his descendants will inherit it."

Pray this verse with your name inserted and ask the Lord to give you fortitude as you follow Him wholeheartedly.

'But because my servant _____ has a different spirit and follows me wholeheartedly, I will bring him/her into the land that he/she is meant to go.'

CONFRONTATIONAL CONVERSATIONS

2 TIMOTHY 2:25-26

"Those who oppose Him He must gently instruct, in the hope that God will grant them repentance leading them to a knowledge of the truth and that they will come to their senses and escape from the trap of the devil, who has taken them captive to do his will."

CHALLENGE:

How do we confront others about deliberate sin while also staying true to God's truth and love?

INSPIRATION:

There have been two times in my life when I had to confront another Christian about a serious sin against God. These confrontations were not made spontaneously. Both times when I felt the Lord leading me to confront, I prayed for His wisdom and discernment. Honestly, I was hoping that I was wrong in what He was leading me to do. Being a person who hates confrontation, I did not want to have these conversations. I even asked the Lord why I had to be the one to confront — why couldn't He ask someone else? He spoke to my spirit and said He asked me because He knew I could be trusted to do it. Thank you, Lord, for trusting me, but this is going to be so hard for me. Ugh!!

This Godly assignment wasn't taken lightly by me. I prayed and prayed and prayed. I even consulted wise counsel to make sure all my words were grounded in God's truth. To say I was afraid would be an understatement. The outcome of one of those conversations could make my life exceedingly difficult. Reactions could be extremely negative.

I remember on one of the days, I texted my friend, Debbie, and asked her to pray for me during the set time of confrontation. I didn't give her any details, just asked her to be praying for me at the specific time. When God calls us to obedience, He will always provide the strength we need and prayers from friends always helps!

Confrontational conversations can be difficult, but we must always remember that they are to be done in a place of love. We should love our brothers and sisters in Christ enough to help steer them back to a righteous relationship with the Savior. We all fall short of His glory. Thankfully, He loves us so much that He will do everything possible to prevent us from staying in the pit of deliberate sin.

I obeyed God and had those difficult conversations. I survived. God was able to trust me. My faith in Him conquered my fear!! The outcome? Well, some friendships were lost for both myself and my family.

God was faithful in His protection of my situation and the reactions and outcome were much better than they could have been. We must remember that Christ doesn't call us to comfort; He calls us to Him even if it means friendships are lost.

GOD'S TRUTH:

Deliberate sin is a dangerous trap and a slippery slope. Paul even tells us in the above verse that Satan has taken people captive to do his will. By ourselves, we are no match for Satan, but we serve a God who can bring us victory from the pit of deliberate sin. God's word is very clear on how we should confront others — always confront in LOVE! We must learn to view confrontation as an act of love — whether we are confronting or being confronted. We must also use God's method of "gentle instruction." Blasting someone on social media is never the answer. Neither is ignoring the entire situation. Confrontation in love is God's gentle way of sending graceful warnings to turn our ways back to Him. Even when people are happy in their life of deliberate sin, God says to hate the sin but love the sinner.

YOUR TRUTH:

Have you ever had to confront someone? Have you ever been the one confronted? Our truth associated with confrontation usually involves a lot of emotions related to the situation. My husband has confronted me about deliberate sin many times. Even though it is extremely irritating at the time, I eventually come to appreciate his concern for my spiritual walk. We must also remember that it is not our goal to give them an escape from the pit or control the outcome. Only God can bring them to repentance and righteousness. Our goal is to pray, confront in love (or be confronted), and pray more.

Is there someone whom God is leading you to confront? Which of God's truths should be shared with him/her?

_____

_____

_____

_____

ACTION PLAN:

1. Pray. God never withholds His wisdom when we ask Him for guidance. Confront in love and without judgment. We are all susceptible to the pit of deliberate sin. If someone confronts you, be grateful that God is sending the message to come back to Him.

Pray Psalm 19:12-13 over your life and the life of your loved ones: "Who can discern his errors? Forgive my hidden faults. Keep your servant also from willful sins; may they not rule over me. Then will I be blameless, innocent of great transgression."

WEEK 4 –
DAILY DEVOTIONS: 2 TIMOTHY

Chapter 3
TRUTHFULLY SPEAKING

2 TIMOTHY 3:1-5

"But mark this: There will be terrible times in the last days. People will be lovers of themselves, lovers of money, boastful, proud, abusive, disobedient to their parents, ungrateful, unholy, without love, unforgiving, slanderous, without self-control, brutal, not lovers of the good, treacherous, rash, conceited, lovers of pleasure rather than lovers of God — having a form of godliness but denying its power. Have nothing to do with them."

CHALLENGE:

How do we remain faithful to God while living in a world of mass corruption?

INSPIRATION:

God never requires us to do the heavy lifting. He is the one who will handle the corruption and bring justice. That is not on our shoulders. He expects us to recognize the evil in our world and be aware of its dangers. The biggest danger is to turn our hearts away from our Savior. As we discussed before, sin is a slippery slope that can prey on its victim in record time. Our inspiration is to keep our eyes on Christ who is always available to strengthen us. Since Paul is describing our current world in the above verses, we must unite with other Christ followers who desire to keep their eyes above. You may be discouraged in thinking that you are the only dedicated Christ follower. Take heart. Ask the Lord to lead you to others who want to share hope. A word of caution — be very discerning whom you follow. As Paul says, have nothing to do with those that have a form of godliness but no power. That means everything on the outside sounds good but underneath there is just power from self, not from Christ. If you aren't sure about a person or his/her message, take it to God and His word. The true message of real Christ followers is that Christ is always at the core.

GOD'S TRUTH:

In the above verses, Paul gives specific examples of corrupt and sinful actions. These actions are easy to identify in ourselves and others. They are just as prevalent in Christians and non-Christians, unfortunately. It's hard to witness so many "Christians" being arrested for corruption, but this is God's truth for our world right now. God will not tolerate hidden sin forever. He wants us in a right relationship with Him and cares too much to let sin keep us captive. Eyes Up, Christ Followers!

YOUR TRUTH:

Of the above sins, which one is your biggest struggle? How does your truth about this sin compare to God's truth?

_____

_____

_____

_____

ACTION PLAN:

1. Break free from negativity especially from news outlets and social media. Your mind can easily become a prison to negativity which is a breeding ground for sin and corruption.

2. Beware of any red flags that the Holy Spirit shows you.

3. Ask God for discernment and protection in finding the right Christ followers to offer hope.

4. Be grateful that God is in complete control — He says to us, "Never will I leave you; never will I forsake you" (Heb. 13:5b).

Study the scriptures and know for yourself what is God's truth. Acts 17:11 says, "Now the Bereans were of more noble character than the Thessalonians, for they received the message with great eagerness and **examined the scriptures every day to see if what Paul said was true.**"

FLAWS AND ALL

2 TIMOTHY 3:6-9:

> "They are the kind who worm their way into homes and gain control over weak-willed women, who are loaded down with sins and are swayed by all kinds of evil desires, always learning but never able to acknowledge the truth. Just as Jannes and Jambres opposed Moses, so also these men oppose the truth — men of depraved minds, who, as far as the faith is concerned, are rejected. But they will not get very far because, as in the case of those men, their folly will be clear to everyone."

CHALLENGE:

How do we not become loaded down with sins and therefore avoid being vulnerable to evil?

Inspiration: Verses 8-9 — *"Just as Jannes and Jambres opposed Moses, so also these men oppose the truth — men of depraved minds, who, as far as the faith is concerned, are rejected. But they will not get very far because, as in the case of those men, their folly will be clear to everyone."*

If you aren't familiar with this story, you can find it in Exodus 7. Moses was chosen by God to lead the Israelites out of Egypt. Pharaoh, the Egyptian leader, didn't want to let the Israelites out of his land. Pharaoh challenged Moses and his brother, Aaron, to a miracle duel. God had told Moses this would happen. There would be miracle contests between Moses and the two Egyptian magicians, Jannes and Jambres.

First Miracle: Aaron's rod turned into a serpent; magicians did the same.

Second Miracle: Moses turned the water into blood; magicians did the same.

Third Miracle: Moses brought up frogs to cover the land; magicians did the same.

Fourth Miracle: Aaron struck the dust of the ground and it turned into gnats; the magicians COULD NOT imitate it.

Warren Wiersbe explains in his book, Be Faithful, "Satan is an imitator; what God does, Satan counterfeits. The religious leaders in the last days will have a counterfeit faith, and their purpose is to promote a lie and resist the truth of God's word. They deny the authority of the Bible and substitute human wisdom and philosophy. In their attempt to be 'modern' they deny the reality of sin and people's need for salvation.

Jannes and Jambres were finally exposed and made fools of by the judgements of God. This will also happen to the leaders of false religions in the last days. When God's judgements fall, the true character of these counterfeits will be revealed to everyone." Hallelujah!!!

GOD'S TRUTH:

God knows that being loaded down with sins will only continue to weaken us and render us useless in defeating it with our own strength. Being loaded down with sin, will leave you emotionally, spiritually, and mentally vulnerable to evil desires. Wiersbe explains, "In Paul's day, women were especially susceptible to this kind of experience since they had a low status in society. Whether men or women, people who fall for this false religious system have the same characteristics. **They are burdened with guilt and looking for some escape from bondage and fear. They find themselves unable to control their various desires."**

Wiersbe continues, "These false religious leaders take advantage of the problems people have and promise them quick and easy solutions. They 'worm their way in' and soon control people's lives. It is not long before these leaders grab their followers' loyalty, money, and service. And their 'converts' are worse off than they were before. They still have their problems, but they have been duped into thinking that all is well. And remember: All of this underhanded activity is done in the name of religion!"

God tells us that Satan has his followers seeking out those loaded down by sin to continue with evil desires. (John 10:10a, "The thief, Satan, comes only to steal, kill, and destroy.") When a person is too focused on himself/herself and ignores the burden of heavy sins, he/she will be more susceptible to the devil's schemes and his web of lies.

The best news is that God does not expect us to fight this battle without Him. We do not have enough strength from our own power to defeat the enemy. God gives us His strength freely to align with Him and be uplifted from the load of sin.

YOUR TRUTH:

What sins and evil desires are loading you down?

_____

_____

_____

_____

ACTION PLAN:

1. Recognize the sin in your life — past and present.

2. Ask God for His forgiveness for the sins in your life.

3. Repent and turn away from those sins and evil desires — Acts 3:19, "Repent, then, and turn to God, so that your sins may be wiped out, that times of refreshing may come from the Lord."

Advice from John MacArthur in his commentary of 2 Timothy,

"<u>First</u>, we must realize that the church is in spiritual warfare, a warfare that will intensify as Christ's second coming draws nearer.

<u>Second</u>, we must be doctrinally discerning, testing every message that claims to be Christian against God's word.

<u>Third</u>, we must be pure and holy vessels of honor for the Lord to use. Christ's own righteousness is our protection against false teachers, false doctrine, and ungodly living.

<u>Fourth</u>, we must be patient, a difficult task for many Christians today who want instant answers to their questions and immediate resolution of their problems. **"Our responsibility is to remain faithful."**

SHARE THE STRUGGLE

2 TIMOTHY 3:10-15

"You, however, know all about my teaching, my way of life, my purpose, faith, patience, love, endurance, persecutions, sufferings — what kinds of things happened to me in Antioch, Iconium and Lystra, the persecutions I endured. Yet the Lord rescued me from all of them. In fact, everyone who wants to live a godly life in Christ Jesus will be persecuted, while evil men and imposters will go from bad to worse, deceiving and being deceived. But as for you, continue in what you have learned and have become convinced of, because you know those from whom you learned it, and how from infancy you have known the holy scriptures, which are able to make you wise for salvation through faith in Jesus Christ."

CHALLENGE:

Should we share our struggles with others?

INSPIRATION:

It was at the end of a school year and the kids were playing on the playground after school while moms were talking. I mentioned that I would be happy to get a break from the school math program (give me liberty, give me death, but don't give me any math to try to understand). My friend, Jennie, said she was surprised to hear me say that because she thought she was the only mom struggling with the math assignments. Then she said something that I'll never forget. She said emphatically, "Why did we go all year and suffer in silence?" Why hadn't we said something to each other sooner so we could have encouraged each other? That day sealed something in our friendship. We no longer held back from each other with the challenges of school and child raising.

I look back at that school year and wonder how it could have been so much better for our families if we had opened our hearts and shared our struggle. Unfortunately, the enemy plagues our minds with lies that no one else shares our same struggle, and no one else cares about our struggle, and no one else would understand our struggle, and people are too busy to help us with our struggle. Lies, lies, and more lies. Of course, the enemy wants to keep us from each other and feel isolated. Remember, God tells us that the enemy's only desire is to kill, steal, and destroy us (John 10:10). By sharing our struggle with the Lord and with others, we open ourselves up to strength, healing, encouragement and resolution. God is always life-giving; Satan is only for life-killing.

I always get emotional when I read Paul's words from verses 10-11, "You, however, know all about my teaching, my way of life, my purpose, faith, patience, love, endurance, persecutions, sufferings — what kinds of things happened to me in Antioch, Iconium and Lystra, the persecutions I endured. Yet the Lord rescued me from all of them." Paul has given all of himself to Timothy — the joys and the struggles. Even though Paul is the mentor, he has opened himself up to become vulnerable with his mentee. They have shared life together.

Paul has been hurt and rejected by many people in his life, but he did not allow that pain to keep him suffering in silence. In teaching others, we must share all of ourselves, not just the good parts. To share our struggle, it must be sharing the good, the bad and the ugly. This is exactly what Jesus did as well as Paul.

GOD'S TRUTH:

God rescued Paul and He will rescue you. It might not be the exact type of rescue that you want, but He is always our deliverer. Psalm 144:2a says, "He is my loving God and my fortress, my stronghold and deliverer."

God does not want us to suffer in silence. He wants us to share our struggle with Him and other Christ followers. He wants us to be vulnerable and open ourselves to His healing and comfort. He wants all of us — the good, the bad, and the ugly. He created us. He knows us better than we know ourselves. He never wants to see his creation turn away from Him.

God also knows that we are relational beings, and He will give us people in our lives to share with. We are to be honest vessels with our struggles to the right people. Hebrews 10:23-25 says, "Let us hold unswervingly to the hope we profess, for He who promised is faithful. And let us consider how we may spur one another on toward love and good deeds. Let us not give up meeting together, as some are in the habit of doing, but let us encourage one another — and all the more as you see the Day approaching."

YOUR TRUTH:

Are you able to share your struggles with others? Why or why not?

Do you encourage others to share their struggle with you? Why or why not?

_____

_____

_____

_____

ACTION PLAN:

1. Share your struggles with God FIRST then others. Other Christ followers are to be in our lives to enhance our relationship with Him, not to replace it.

2. Ask God who you should share your struggle with. He will lead you to the right person.

3. Start small — ask others if they have any tips for any challenges you are having. Most people are willing to help and share.

4. Remember that Paul had many to reject him initially, but God brought Timothy in his life who was a faithful friend to the end.

DOES THE BIBLE HAVE ALL THE ANSWERS TO OUR PROBLEMS?

2 TIMOTHY 3:16-17

"All scripture is God-breathed and is useful for teaching, rebuking, correcting, and training in righteousness, so that the man of God may be thoroughly equipped for every good work."

CHALLENGE:

Does the Bible have all the answers to our problems?

INSPIRATION:

One day I asked my husband if he saw the glass half full or half empty? He said it depended on what was in the glass! I laughed out loud at my witty hubby. So funny!

With God, He wants us to realize that it doesn't matter what is in the glass because He wants us to be filled with Him.

In the Old Testament, a prophet named Jeremiah was told by God to "take a scroll and write on it all the words I have spoken to you concerning Israel, Judah and all the other nations from the time I began speaking to you in the reign of Josiah till now" (Jer. 36:2). This was twenty-two years' worth of information to be written down! Not an easy task. God tells Jeremiah the purpose of this assignment in verse three,

"Perhaps when the people of Judah hear about every disaster I plan to inflict on them, each of them will turn from his wicked way; then I will forgive their wickedness and their sin."

God had made it clear to His people that He wanted them focused on Him and only Him. Jeremiah obeyed God in this assignment and dictated the words to his scribe, Baruch, and together they completed the scroll. The Bible does not tell us how long this process took, but we can be sure that it was a lot of time and effort from these two Godly men.

Jeremiah then instructed Baruch to go to the house of the Lord and read the scroll to the people in hopes that they would repent of their wicked ways and turn to the Lord.

Unfortunately for Jeremiah and Baruch, their ungodly king, Jehoiakim, did not want to hear God's words that were written on the scroll. After the king had heard three or four columns, he threw the entire scroll into the fire pot and it was destroyed. Jehoiakim, the king, commanded that Jeremiah and Baruch be arrested but "the Lord had hidden them" (Jer. 36:26).

God spoke to Jeremiah again, "Take another scroll and write on it all the words that were on the first scroll, which Jehoiakim king of Judah burned up. Also tell Jehoiakim king of Judah, 'This is what the Lord says: Since you burned that scroll, you will have no one to sit on the throne of David; your body will be thrown out and exposed to the heat by day and the frost by night. I will punish you and your children and your attendants for their wickedness; I will bring on them and those living in Jerusalem and the people of Judah every disaster I pronounced against them, because they have not listened'" (Jer. 36:28-31).

Jeremiah instructed Baruch to take another scroll and write down all the words that he dictated. Ugh! Can you imagine? Twenty-two years of information to be handwritten all over again. Why would God have the men repeat all that work? I would have hated to repeat that assignment, but these two men did not focus on the glass being half empty.

God knew that His words would be life giving. Jeremiah and Baruch did not focus on the glass being half empty. Instead they focused on God and obeyed His instructions because of the love they had for Him.

I hope Baruch is in heaven getting a hand massage!!

GOD'S TRUTH:

God tells us in the Bible that His words are useful for teaching, rebuking, correcting, and training in righteousness so we are equipped for any problems that arise. Not only does God give us the answers to our problems but also how to use those answers to work in our lives.

YOUR TRUTH:

Are you currently more focused on what's in your glass or on the Lord? What truth are you using to equip you? Do you choose the world's truth, emotions, critical thinking and circumstances or do you choose God's truth?

_____

_____

_____

_____

ACTION PLAN:

1. Identify your problem.

2. Ask the Holy Spirit to direct you on where to look in the Bible for answers.

3. Search the concordance in the back of the Bible by key words.

4. Read verses in context (read the surrounding verses to get the entire meaning of what God is saying).

5. God's words hold the answers, so trust His direction.

WEEK 5 –
DAILY DEVOTIONS: 2 TIMOTHY

Chapter 4
REACH AND TEACH

2 TIMOTHY 4:1-5

"In the presence of God and of Christ Jesus, who will judge the living and the dead, and in view of His appearing and His kingdom, I give you this charge: Preach the Word; be prepared in season and out of season; correct, rebuke and encourage — with great patience and careful instruction, for the time will come when men will not put up with sound doctrine. Instead, to suit their own desires, they will gather around them a great number of teachers to say what their itching ears want to hear. They will turn their ears away from the truth and turn aside to myths. But you, keep your head in all situations, endure hardship, do the work of an evangelist, discharge all the duties of your ministry."

CHALLENGE:

What are our duties as a disciple for Christ?

INSPIRATION:

Too often Christ followers get stuck on what their calling is when God is more concerned with our spreading the gospel message. Here is the great news — the Holy Spirit is always available to assist us. Very simply, God wants us to use our unique story to share with others and give God the glory.

There is no script we have to memorize or facts to recite. Through our experiences, we can show love to others and point them to our Savior. Jesus Christ, our Savior, is the ONLY answer for eternal salvation. By sharing our life story with others, we can testify how God has strengthened our lives to make us disciples for His truth.

Ephesians 1:13-14, "And you also were included in Christ when you heard the word of truth, the gospel of your salvation. Having believed, you were marked in Him with a seal, the promised Holy Spirit, who is a deposit guaranteeing our inheritance until the redemption of those who are God's possession — to the praise of His glory."

What glorious rewards for us. God adopted us, Jesus redeemed us, and the Holy Spirit sealed us. This is the great news to share with others!

More great news in 1 John 5:3: "This is love for God: to obey His commands. And His commands are not burdensome." The Lord even makes it easier on us by telling us that His burdens are not heavy. Part of our job as a disciple is to show our foundation of faith in God when circumstances are hard. Others are always watching Christ followers either to see hypocrisy or hope. Let's be a true disciple and show them our hope is in our Savior, Jesus Christ.

GOD'S TRUTH:

False doctrine has become an epidemic in our country. Many 'pastors and evangelists' have become extremely wealthy by telling people what they want their itching ears to hear, BUT it is not aligned with God's truth. In his book, *Christian Excellence*, John Johnstone, says, "Success is attaining cultural goals that elevate one's importance in the eyes of society and generally is marked by power, prestige, wealth, and privilege. Excellence is the pursuit of the highest quality in one's work and effort whether others recognize and approve it or not. Success is measured in relation to others, whereas excellence is measured by one's own God-given potential and calling. Success seeks to please men; excellence seeks to please God."

Paul is clearly emphasizing these same thoughts to Timothy and to us. Choose to please your Savior over your worldly success AND encourage others to do the same. Reach and Teach. Share and Care.

YOUR TRUTH:

What kind of disciple are you to others? Is it clear to everyone in your circle how much you love Jesus?

_____

_____

_____

_____

ACTION PLAN:

Paul gives us the best action plan to use in his writing to Timothy:

1. Preach the word.

2. Be prepared in season and out of season.

3. Correct, rebuke, encourage with great patience and careful instruction.

4. Keep your head in all situations.

5. Endure hardship.

6. Do the work of an evangelist.

7. Fulfill all duties of your ministry (keep God first).

FAITH TO FINISH

2 TIMOTHY 4:6-8

"For I am already being poured out like a drink offering, and the time has come for my departure. I have fought the good fight, I have finished the race, I have kept the faith. Now there is in store for me the crown of righteousness, which the Lord, the righteous Judge, will award to me on that day — and not only to me, but also to all who have longed for His appearing."

CHALLENGE:

How do we finish strong in the faith?

INSPIRATION:

Paul knew he was at the end of his life. He would soon be moving to heaven and meeting his Savior. Paul shows us what it's like to finish our life strong and faithful. He is confident of his time on earth and has full expectation to receive the crown of righteousness.

James 1:12 says, "Blessed is the man who perseveres under trial, because when he has stood the test, he will receive the crown of life that God has promised to those who love Him."

As God's children, He will reward us with crowns in heaven according to our actions on earth. This is different from salvation which is not based on our actions but on faith through grace in Jesus Christ. Once Jesus has become our Savior, our actions reveal who we are truly living for — Jesus or ourselves.

There's no mistaking that Paul lived his life completely for Jesus. His passion and faithfulness even in the darkest of circumstances gave him confidence in knowing that he would receive the crown of righteousness in heaven.

Jesus promises us rewards and crowns in heaven for different actions on earth. One of those is the crown of righteousness for those that long to be with the Lord in eternity. For Christ followers, dying and being in Heaven is so much better than this earth. Jesus wants us to desire heaven more than we want to stay on earth.

Our goal should be the same as Paul: fight the good fight and finish the race faithfully.

GOD'S TRUTH:

Jesus was the ultimate faithful finisher. For Him to finish strong, He had to endure brutality and extreme physical pain and suffering. Not only did Jesus know this was to happen, but He surrendered His mind and body to His Father's will for this to happen. Jesus endured it all just so you and I could live in eternity with Him. While on earth, Jesus had one mission: to tell the truth of God's love and how eternal salvation is available for all who choose Him as Savior.

God wants us to finish strong and He gives His strength freely to us in order to do that. There were so many times I wandered away from God. In the dark pit of depression, I didn't know who I was, much less who God was. I didn't even know how to pray. It was like my mind was full of mud with no clarity or hope to be found.

There will be times when you don't know how to pray. The most important thing is to be prepared for these times BEFORE they happen. We will discuss these preparations in the action plan. Right now, it is imperative to know that God's truth is that He always sees our struggles, understands our struggles, and provides His Holy Spirit to help us through our struggles.

We will consistently be pulled and pushed by the enemy to turn our backs on God. There will even be times when it seems this is the easier thing to do. BUT a faithful finisher knows that he/she will often stumble but God will never let him/her fall.

Psalm 37:23-24 says, "If the Lord delights in a man's way, He makes his steps firm; though he stumble, he will not fall, for the Lord upholds him with His hand."

Rejoice, rejoice — God holds us up and doesn't let us fall!!!

YOUR TRUTH:

Our human nature often leads us into the wrong direction. We allow emotions, thoughts, past experiences, and circumstances to lead our steps. We can easily convince ourselves that following Christ is too hard and it's not worth it. My friend, THIS IS NOT GOD'S TRUTH. His love for us is so much more than we can imagine. He wants us to be faithful finishers and even gives us His divine help to do it!

Your Truth: What is your mindset when you want to quit? How does your truth about giving up compare to God's truth to finish strong?

_____

_____

_____

_____

ACTION PLAN:

To have a faithful finish and to finish strong, we MUST have the mindset of Christ. Christ's mind was consistently focused on His father's will. The more we draw closer to Him, the more we will have His mindset. However, there will be those times when our human nature prevails, and we are emotionally paralyzed by our emotions, thoughts and circumstances. To prepare for those times, it is best to put 3 things in your truth tool kit.

1. Prayer Partner: this is someone that you make an agreement with to pray for you when you can't pray for yourself. This is a person that you can send a message to ask for prayer without having to give all the details. Our prayer partners don't always need to know the details because God already knows them. Your prayer partner should be a person that you know is committed to praying for you when you ask her to.

2. Truth Mantra: I will finish strong!! Put this in your head to repeat repeatedly. Write it on a notecard to put on your mirror, refrigerator, and in your car. Speak it until you believe it.

3. Scripture, Scripture, Scripture: The Bible is God's gift to help us know His truth and have His mindset.

4. Memorize these verses to allow the Holy Spirit to infuse them with power needed to finish strong!

    Acts 20:24 says, "However, I consider my life worth nothing to me, if only I may finish the race and complete the task the Lord Jesus has given me — the task of testifying to the gospel of God's grace."

    Psalm 119:165 says, "Great peace have they who love your law, and nothing can make them stumble."

    Proverbs 3:21-26 says, "My son, preserve sound judgment and discernment, do not let them out of your sight; they will be life for you, an ornament to grace your neck. Then you will go on your way in safety, and your foot will not stumble; when you lie down, your sleep will be sweet. Have no fear of sudden disaster or of the ruin that overtakes the wicked, for the Lord will be your confidence and will keep your foot from being snared."

THE FIGHT TO NOT FALL AWAY

2 TIMOTHY 4:9-13

"Do your best to come to me quickly, for Demas, because he loved this world, has deserted me and has gone to Thessalonica. Crescens has gone to Galatia, and Titus to Dalmatia. Only Luke is with me. Get Mark and bring him with you, because he is helpful to me in my ministry. I sent Tychicus to Ephesus. When you come, bring the cloak that I left with Carpus at Troas, and my scrolls, especially the parchments."

CHALLENGE:

How can we not fall away from God and His plans for our life?

As we read the verses above, we understand that Paul is telling Timothy that there will be faithful ones as well as unfaithful ones. Paul mentions Demas who was one of his ministry companions four years earlier. Demas deserted Paul, the ministry and Christ for his worldly endeavors.

Crescens and Titus were still faithful but serving in other areas to spread the gospel. Paul had Luke with him who was a wonderful blessing to him. Paul also wanted to see Mark and Timothy since he knew that he was living his last days in prison.

So, what makes one person remain faithful and another person to fail?

INSPIRATION:

God gives each of His children a special gift that is unique to them. This gift is to be used for His glory and for His kingdom. Ephesians 2:10 tells us, "For we are God's workmanship, created in Christ Jesus to do good works, which God prepared in advance for us to do." Doesn't it blow your mind that God planned our gifts before we even were created? If we obey Him, He will direct every step we take toward fulfilling our gifts for His glory. Proverbs 16:3 says, "Commit to the Lord whatever you do, and your plans will succeed."

With believers, however, there seem to be two problems. First, we are often too busy pursuing worldly endeavors to realize we are in danger of falling further and further away from God. Second, we get frustrated with God because He doesn't move fast enough with what we think should happen.

For the first category:

God gives us each a specific love and passion for certain cultural area(s) in which we can use His strength to make a difference in this world. We all have Godly missions to expand His kingdom; however, too many of us ignore those missions or let the world dictate what is most important. All our missions should point to Christ — not ourselves. If your passion is to feed hungry children, then how can you accomplish that mission to give God all the glory? What makes you different than an unbeliever who is passionate to feed hungry children? As God's children, we are called to share and show the love of Christ in everything that we do.

For the second category, let me share my story.

I had three babies in four years. In their young years, my sanity was questionable. It was so hard. Older women in my church would see me with three young kids in tow and tell me "oh, I remember those days." I hated hearing that because I always thought to myself — well, if you truly remembered those days then you would be offering to come to my house and help me. And don't get me started with all the women who would see me pregnant and tell me how much they loved being pregnant. I always wanted to slap those women in the face — in Jesus' Name. All my pregnancies were extremely difficult to say the least. The last thing I wanted to hear was about another woman's super easy pregnancy.

Save it. Tell it to someone who cares. Certainly not my best Christ-filled moments!

In today's culture, being a stay-at-home mom is not good enough. The world dictates to us that we should also be blogging, YouTubing, volunteering, having a side business, serving on committees, working in ministry or writing books. Why can't we just focus on our babies? None of the other things are bad, but are we doing them because it's God's will at the time or because we are following the world's dictates? I totally get it. I've been there so many times. At times, motherhood was so hard that I wanted to focus on something else. Through the years, I juggled several different missions. Some of them were God's will and some of them weren't. Often, I wanted an escape from the daily grind of motherhood. I also wanted to still feel important and accomplished even though I smelled like baby milk most of the time. I wanted more adult interaction to stimulate my brain. I wanted to feel connected to other women.

As my children have grown, I regret the plates that I juggled that weren't in God's will. Why couldn't I ignore the world and let motherhood be enough? Why couldn't I enjoy the season with young kids without convincing myself that I needed more? Why did I fall away from God's planned path for my life?

GOD'S TRUTH:

The beauty of being in God's will is that He completely understands the season that you are in. He knows what we can handle and what we can't. God knows our hearts, our passions, and desires. He also knows the perfect timing to pursue those. I have always dreamed of being a public speaker, even taking steps toward that dream without God's permission. God had given me the dream and the talent, so shouldn't I be pursuing it as much as possible? Yes and no. We must be clear on God's timing and direction for our passions and dreams. Pursuing this dream while my kids were little was certainly not God's timing. I'm so grateful for His protection of closing doors during my stubborn selfishness. I can see now that His timing is perfect; every dream and passion has its right season. With God's delay of this dream, I was still able to grow and learn in areas that would help me be a better speaker and most importantly a more obedient daughter to Him. I was able to fan into the flame of His presence, trusting Him fully to learn what I needed to before moving on.

God wants each of us to remain faithful to Him while we wait for His perfect timing. This could mean sitting in His presence and listening to His voice. It could be studying His word and memorizing scripture. It could mean worshiping Him even in difficult circumstances. It could mean starting to write a business plan for pursuing your dream.

Let's remember that Paul took three years to be in God's presence before starting his ministry. Jesus took thirty years to be in His father's presence before beginning His three year ministry. Our first responsibility is to fan into the flame by being in God's presence. We must prioritize the time to soak up His wisdom and direction. He will always let us know when it's time to move. Remember — God's preparation before your planning.

YOUR TRUTH:

Was there a time in your life that you fell away from God? Why do think that happened? How can you strengthen your relationship with Christ, so you don't fall away from Him?

_____

_____

_____

_____

ACTION PLAN:

No matter where you are with your relationship with Christ, the formula is the same to remain faithful: **Abide, Avow, Align**

Step 1: ABIDE — to act in accordance with

In the book *Abide in Christ* by Andrew Murray, he tells us exactly what it means to abide. "It takes time to grow in Jesus the Vine (John 15); do not expect to abide in Him unless you will give Him that time. It is not enough to read God's word, or meditations offered here and, when we think we have hold of the thoughts and have asked God for His blessing, then go out in the hope that the blessing will abide. No, it requires time with Jesus and with God day by day. We all know the time required for our meals each day. If we are to live through Jesus, we must feed on Him (John 6:57). Therefore, if you want to learn to abide in Jesus, take time each day to put yourself into living contact with the living Jesus, to yield yourself distinctly and consciously to His blessed influence. By doing so, you will give Him the opportunity of taking hold of you, of drawing you up and keeping you safe in His almighty life."

Simply put — Abide = Daily time with Jesus through prayer and His word. We cannot find our flame or fan it without first abiding in Christ.

Step 2: AVOW — to assert, confess openly, and acknowledge

Once you have the foundation of abiding in Christ, He will lead you to avow your gift. I love the word avow. The word reminds us that we have a binding vow with our Lord to go forth and build His kingdom. With our obedience to Him, He graciously leads us each step of the way. God is not likely to lay out the entire plan for your life. He wants us to trust Him and His timing. When we avow our spiritual flame, we open the doors for God to move on our behalf. Even with challenges, He is there for us to rely on Him to overcome. His way is the best way. To me, this stage is mostly a mental mindset. We choose to follow Christ in the process of our journey despite our feelings, insecurities, or burdens. To avow is about Him, not us. "The Sovereign Lord is my strength; He makes my feet like the feet of a deer; He enables me to go on the heights" (Hab. 3:19).

Step 3: ALIGN — to be in a state of agreement

Once we have our mental mind set to avow, we are ready to align ourselves with the Lord. This means we are ready to work towards His plan for us. We agree with His will even though we don't know the entire picture. At this step, it doesn't matter where God leads us because we know it's all in our best interest. "And we know that all things work together for good to those who love God, to those who are called according to His purpose" (Rom. 8:28). Our alignment with God allows us to put our spiritual gifts to action. If He opens a door, we walk through. If He closes a door, we wait for Him to open another one.

Abide, Avow, Align

BITTER FROM BETRAYAL

2 TIMOTHY 4:14-18

"Alexander the metalworker did me a great deal of harm. The Lord will repay him for what he has done. You too should be on your guard against him, because he strongly opposed our message. At my first defense, no one came to my support, but everyone deserted me. May it not be held against them. But the Lord stood at my side and gave me strength, so that through me the message might be fully proclaimed, and all the Gentiles might hear it. And I was delivered from the lion's mouth. The Lord will rescue me from every evil attack and will bring me safely to His heavenly kingdom. To Him be glory for ever and ever. Amen."

CHALLENGE:

How do you not become consumed with bitterness when others betray you?

INSPIRATION:

Have you ever heard the phrase "get better, not bitter"? I've always loved that phrase, but I don't think there's a harder phrase than this one to live out. A deep betrayal can crash your world and put you in the pits of earthly hell like nothing else.

The Bible is certainly not lacking in stories of betrayal. Betrayals that led to wars, murder, and destruction. Thankfully, there's also a message of hope and renewal that can rise up from the ashes of betrayal.

Let's look at three biblical examples of how betrayal led to becoming better instead of bitter.

1. **Samson**: In Judges 16, we learn the story of the judge, Samson. God had given Samson amazing strength if no razor was used on his head. Samson's wife, Delilah, was offered a lot of money from the Philistines to find out the secret to Samson's strength. To say that Delilah nagged him to tell her is an understatement. Judges 16:16 tells us "with such nagging she prodded him day after day until he was tired to death." Delilah wasted no time in cutting Samson's hair while he slept and alerting the Philistines. They captured him and took him as a prisoner.

   It's important for us to know that not all the blame fell on Delilah and the Philistines. Before this incident, Samson had fallen out of obedience to God and lived according to his own worldly desires. He was no longer in alignment with God's direction for his life. After the betrayal, Samson realized his fatal mistake. Instead of playing the blame game, Samson allowed his bitterness to bring him back to God. <u>For Samson, *the betrayal brought repentance and a renewed relationship with God*.</u>

2. **Paul**: Unfortunately, Paul was no stranger to betrayal. There were many in his life that turned away from him and the faith. He shares with Timothy in the above verses that Alexander had done him a great deal of harm. Paul also had talked about others in previous verses who had deserted him. Paul had every reason to be bitter from these betrayals, but he chose to stay focused on what mattered most. He clearly tells Timothy that the Lord will handle the people who had done wrong. Paul did not consider it his place to deal with the betrayals. He writes two especially important sentences that we should also use in our life: a) "The Lord will repay them for what they have done," b) "May it not be held against them." Instead of getting distracted by the bitterness, Paul gave it over to the Lord so he could continue to focus on the mission of the gospel. <u>*For Paul, the betrayals brought a renewed sense of purpose and commitment to his calling of spreading the gospel*.</u>

3. **Jesus**: There's no one who understands betrayal more than Jesus. He had the betrayal of the whole world on Him when He died on the cross for all our sins. In His three years of ministry, He would constantly encounter betrayals and rejections from those listening to His message who wanted to stone Him for blasphemy. Probably these betrayals did not hurt nearly as much as the ones from those closest to Him. One of His twelve disciples, Judas, betrayed Him by turning Him over to the Roman soldiers. Another disciple, Peter, betrayed Jesus by denying Him three different times. The Jews, Jesus' own people, betrayed Him by telling Pilate to have Him crucified. Heartbroken, Jesus remained faithful to His purpose. He never became distracted by the pain of the betrayal. He followed His Father's instructions to the bitter end. <u>*For Jesus, the betrayals brought forgiveness of sins, salvation and eternal life for all who believe*.</u>

GOD'S TRUTH:

Deuteronomy 31:6 says, "Be strong and courageous. Do not be afraid or terrified because of them, for the Lord your God goes with you; He will never leave you nor forsake you."

<u>Others will betray us, but God never will.</u>

Samson's betrayal brought repentance of sins and renewed relationship.

Paul's betrayal brought the Lord's strength to finish his mission.

Jesus' betrayal brought forgiveness, salvation, and eternal life for all to receive.

YOUR TRUTH:

What betrayal do you have that can be given to the Lord in order to change from bitter to better?

_____

_____

_____

_____

ACTION PLAN:

Paul gives us the perfect action plan in His letter to Timothy.

1. Be on guard against those who oppose the gospel message. "Be on guard against him because he strongly opposed our message" (verse 15).

2. Let the Lord handle everyone who betrays you. Give it to Him and don't take it back! "The Lord will repay him for what he has done" (verse 14).

3. Practice forgiveness. "May it not be held against them" (verse 16).

4. Draw strength from the Lord. "But the Lord stood at my side and gave me strength" (verse 17).

5. Do not let the betrayal distract you from your Godly mission. Your call is to be completed. "So that through me the message might be fully proclaimed" (verse 17).

FINAL WORDS: WHERE WILL YOU GO (SPEL)?

2 TIMOTHY 4:19-22

> "Greet Priscilla and Aquila and the household of Onesiphorus. Erastus stayed in Corinth, and I left Trophimus sick in Miletus. Do your best to get here before winter. Eubulus greets you, and so do Pudens, Linus, Claudia and the brothers. The Lord be with your spirit. Grace be with you."

CHALLENGE:

Where will you GO (spel)?

INSPIRATION:

The above verses are the last words written from Paul to Timothy. Paul had so much betrayal in his life but it's comforting to know that his last thoughts were on the people who had not deserted him.

In Warren Wiersbe's book, *Be Faithful*, he gives us a wonderful synopsis of Paul's life.

"What a man! His friends forsake him, and he prays that God will forgive them. His enemies try him, and he looks for opportunities to tell them how to be saved! What a difference it makes when the Holy Spirit controls your life."

"Paul's greatest fear was not of death; it was that he might deny his Lord or do something else that would disgrace God's name. Paul was certain that the time had come for his permanent departure. He wanted to end his life-race well and be free from any disobedience."

"You and I must be faithful so that future generations may hear the gospel and have the opportunity to be saved."

GOD'S TRUTH:

As we conclude our devotions on 2 Timothy, we have learned that the most important things to God are our relationship with Him and sharing His redemption message to others. We often become too consumed with ourselves and our circumstances that we don't prioritize the act of sharing the gospel. Jesus is alive in us. We are His children. We can join with Him in sharing our stories with others in order to bring them to know Jesus better. Our responsibility is to love others and share the message. God's responsibility is to prepare their hearts, forgive their sins, and claim them as His own. Sharing is caring!

YOUR TRUTH:

What is your story? How has God worked in your life? Your story is to be used to help others and encourage them that God's love isn't conditional. How can the truth of your life story be used to share the gospel message?

_____

_____

ACTION PLAN:

1. Become clear on your testimony story. This is your personal message to share with others how God has done amazing work in your life. Remember, that each person's story is different. Stories aren't to be compared to others. Our story is to point others to our Savior, Jesus Christ.

2. Be prepared to share your testimony story in any circumstance. There are so many people hurting in this world. As Christ followers, we want to bring hope to a hopeless world. Our personal story combined with the story of Jesus Christ can help bring healing to people who desperately need a Savior.

3. Love others unconditionally. We will never be able to love each other with a perfect love, but we continually strive to love others like Jesus loves them. By loving others (even the hard to love people in our lives), we can share the gospel message without saying any words. We have heard that actions speak louder than words. If we strive to do this on a regular basis, the gospel message will be spoken loud and clear.

As we read Paul's last words, let's be encouraged to move forward with the Holy Spirit and be unafraid and unashamed. Let us join as one body of Christ to GO and share the GOSPEL.

Where will you GO (spel)?

Bibliography

Adam, Peter. *Speaking God's Words* (Leicester, England: InterVarsity Press, 1996)

Barclay, William. *Letters to Timothy, Titus, and Philemon.* (Louisville, KY: Westminister John Knox Press, 2011)

Bernard, J. H. "The Pastoral Epistles," (Grand Rapids, Michigan: Baker, 1980)

Constable, Thomas L. *Notes on Second Timothy.* Sonic Light, 2019 edition

Earle, Ralph. "1&2 Timothy," *The Expositors Bible Commentary, Vol. 11* (Grand Rapids, Michigan: Zondervan, 1981)

Eberstadt, Mary. *It's Dangerous to Believe: Religious Freedom and Its Enemies*, (New York: Harper Collins, 2016) Kindle.

Erickson, Milliard. *Christian Theology*, (Baker Academic: Grand Rapids, Michigan, 2013), Adobe Digital Editions.

Fee Gordon D. "1 and 2 Timothy, Titus," *New International Biblical Commentary* (Peabody, Massachusetts: Hendrickson Publishers, 1993)

Frame, John M. "The Doctrine of God," *A Theology of Worship*, Vol. 4 (Phillipsburg, N.J.: P&R Publishing Company, 2010) Kindle.

Grudem, Wayne. *Systematic Theology: An Introduction to Biblical Doctrine* (Zondervan, Grand Rapids, Michigan, 2015), p. 62-87.

Gundry, Robert H. *Commentary on First and Second Timothy, Titus* (Baker Academics: Grand Rapids, Michigan, 2010) Adobe Digital Editions.

Hendrickson, William. *New Testament Commentary: Exposition of the Pastoral Epistles*, (Grand Rapids: Baker Book House, 1968)

Hiebert, D. Edmond. "Second Timothy," *Everyman's Bible Commentary* (Chicago: Moody Bible Institute, 1958) Kindle.

Hughes, R. Kent. "1-2 Timothy and Titus," *Preaching the Word* (Wheaton, Illinois: Crossway, 2012) Kindle.

Johnston, Jon. *Christian Excellence.* (Lulu.com: 2008)

Knight, George W., III. "The Pastoral Epistles: A Commentary on the Greek Text, *New International Greek Commentary Series,* (Grand Rapids, Michigan: William B. Eerdmans Publishing Co., 1992)

Langbridge, Frederick. *A Cluster of Quiet Thoughts*, (London: The Religious Tract Society, 1886)

Lea, Thomas, D. and Wayne P. Griffin Jr. "First and Second Timothy, Titus", *The New American Commentary, Vol. 34* (Nashville, Tennessee: B&H Publishing Co.,1992) Adobe Digital Editions.

Lock, Walter. *The Pastoral Epistles* (Edinburgh: T&T Clark, 1936.)

MacArthur Jr, John. *The MacArthur New Testament Commentary 2 Timothy.* (Chicago, IL: Moody Publishers, 1995)

Montague, George T. "First and Second Timothy, Titus," *Catholic Commentary on Sacred Scripture* (Grand Rapids, Michigan: Baker Academic, 2008) Adobe Digital Editions.

Mounce, William D. "Second Timothy," *Word Biblical Commentary: Pastoral Epistles*, Vol. 46, (Grand Rapids, Michigan: Zondervan, 2006) Adobe Digital Editions.

Murray, Andrew. *Abide in Christ*. (New Kensington, PA: Whitaker House, 1979)

Oden, Thomas C. "First and Second Timothy and Titus" *Interpretation: A Biblical Commentary for Teaching and Preaching* (Louisville: John Knox Press, 1981), Adobe Digital Editions.

Omokri, Reno. *Leah Sharibu: The Girl Boko Haram Left Behind.* (Kingwood, TX: RevMedia, 2018)

Packer, J. I. *Concise Theology*, (Carol Stream, Illinois: Tyndale House Publishers, 1993).

Stott, J. R. "The Message of Second Timothy" (*The Bible Speaks Today*, Leicester, England: Inter-Varsity Press, 1973)

Towner, Philip H. "The Letters to Timothy and Titus", *The New International Commentary*, (Grand Rapids, Michigan: William B. Eerdmans Publishing Company, 2006) Kindle

Wax, Kevin. *Counterfeit Gospels: Rediscovering the Good News in a World of False Hope* (Chicago, Illinois: Moody Publishers, 2011)

White, R. E. O. "Sanctification." *Evangelical Dictionary of Theology,* 3rd Edition, edited by Daniel J. Treier and Walter A. Elwell, (Baker Academic, 2017) Adobe Digital Editions

Winder Jr., Stanton G. and Kimberly Allston. *When Faith Is All There Is: Faith Is Enough*, (Amazon, 2017.)

Wiersbe, Warren. *Be Faithful.* (Colorado Springs, CO: Cook Communications, 2005)

Wright, N. T. Paul for Everyone: *The Pastoral Letters – First and Second Timothy and Titus.* Louisville, Kentucky: Westminster John Knox Press, 2004.

About the Authors

Stanton Winder and Kimberly Allston have been friends and co-laborers in gospel ministry for fifteen years. Together they have authored *When Faith Is All There Is: Faith Is Enough - An Ancient Prophet Speaks to Today's World* — a part in-depth biblical study, part interactive devotional sharing and inspirational journey of perseverance and hope in the face of injustice.

Kimberly Allston is a wife, mother, and long-time student and teacher of Scripture. She has a bachelor's degree from the College of Charleston and a master's degree from the University of South Carolina. Kimberly has worked with women and women's groups for over twenty years. Kimberly is the founder of Real Connection Ministry and possesses a passion to help women cultivate meaningful connections to Jesus, others, and themselves. She loves to travel, eat chocolate, and participate in sprint triathlons. Kimberly lives in South Carolina with her husband and three children. To connect with Kimberly, visit www.realconnectionministry.com

Stanton Winder is a father, husband, retired ordained minister of nearly twenty years, and a former teacher in Biblical studies and systematic theology at both Bible institutes and Lancaster Bible College. He has also taught English, ESL, Literature, and History in private schools. Stanton has a bachelor's degree from Lancaster Bible College and a master's degree from Biblical Theological Seminary in Biblical Studies. Stanton lives with his wife Sue and five rescue dogs in South Carolina.

CPSIA information can be obtained
at www.ICGtesting.com
Printed in the USA
LVHW080723280321
682721LV00004B/27